UNDER CONSTRUCTION

REFRAMING MEN'S SPIRITUALITY

GARETH BRANDT

Herald Press
Waterloo, Ontario
Scottdale, Pennsylvania

Library and Archives Canada Cataloging in Publication
Brandt, Gareth, 1961-
  Under construction : reframing men's spirituality / Gareth
Brandt.

ISBN 978-0-8361-9502-6
  1. Men (Christian theology). 2. Christian men—Religious
life. I. Title.

BT703.5.B73 2009   248.8'42   C2009-906789-7

The publication of this book was made possible through
funding from Mennonite Men, a binational organization of
Mennonite Church Canada and Mennonite Church USA.

UNDER CONSTRUCTION
Copyright © 2009 by Herald Press, Waterloo, Ont. N2L 6H7
  Published simultaneously in the United States of America
  by Herald Press, Scottdale, Pa. 15683. All rights reserved
Library of Congress Control Number: 2009940645
Canadiana Entry Number: C2009-906789-7
International Standard Book Number: 978-0-8361-9502-6
Printed in the United States of America
Cover design by Merrill R. Miller

13 12 11 10 09   10 9 8 7 6 5 4 3 2 1

To order or request information please call 1-800-245-7894
or visit www.heraldpress.com.

To my beloved sons,
Joel, Adriel, and Micah

CONTENTS

FOREWORD

God, I want somebody to tell me, answer if you can!
Won't somebody tell me, just what is the soul of a man?
—Blind Willie Johnson, 1897-1945

Asking about the soul of a *man* or questing for male spirituality were not questions I heard as a child, teenager, or even early on as a young adult. If someone spoke of the "soul of a *man*," we'd assume they meant the term generically. Back then it was common for people to speak of "man"—as in "man-made"—to include all humans, men or women. As we listened to emerging feminist insights, many men learned to exercise more caution with language and also realized that men had had a lot to say for a long, long time and were entering an era where we should be more reticent. Others began to speak of a growing "men's movement"; responses varied, including a best-selling book that insisted that *Real Men Don't Eat Quiche*.

I am not the only one who experienced confusion and anxiety during such shifts and transitions. Growing up, none of the men whom I knew talked about what it meant to be a *man*. They were not especially introspective, and most of them struggled long and hard just to survive— through the Depression, the Nazi occupation, fighting in wars, and the penury of immigration. Souls? They were

9

happy to feed, house, and clothe their own bodies and the bodies of those they loved.

There were other challenges as I pondered growing into a man. I was bookish and introverted, a reflective dreamer. And the hard-working entrepreneurial men I knew smoked, drank, and cursed. They spoke passionately of cars, hockey, fishing, and earning big bucks. I suspected that I was not a real man long before I ever even heard of a food called quiche.

Later, though, I kept bumping into "men's issues." An older man introduced me to Robert Bly's *Iron John*, but that did not compute. I went to a therapist about an inexplicable depression, and he spent all our time—sessions for which I was paying plenty—trying to convince me to join him and a group of men in the woods, where we could beat drums and our chests, holler, and do who knows what. I did not go with him to the woods, nor did I return for any more sessions. And I wondered whether we really needed a *men's* movement.

Hadn't the Crusades been a men's movement? And the Civil War and the Second World War and the Vietnam War? We men had our messy fingerprints in all kinds of unseemly places and circumstances. Did a men's movement merely mean that the privilege of old boys' networks of smoky back rooms had migrated to the woods or Promise Keepers' stadiums?

Yet something kept niggling at me. As I grew more and more interested in the spiritual practices of the Christian faith, I wondered why women outnumbered men in churches I served, at retreats I attended or led, and in courses on prayer I taught.

In the middle of all this, a favorite Canadian singer, Bruce Cockburn, released an album where he explored the "soul of a man." For numerous years I thought he had written the words quoted above. While the haunting lyrics were often on my mind, and while Cockburn himself had long inspired and challenged me, I was not sure that he could tell me how to be a man. On that particular album Cockburn boasted of a fondness for guns, for example. Prior to that, I felt sad about his string of broken relationships. (More recently, I was astonished to see this social justice advocate apparently endorsing Canada's military efforts in Afghanistan, even to the point of playing with a rocket launcher.)

Only years later did I learn that "What is the soul of a man?" is by the Reverend Blind Willie Johnson. Johnson blended blues and spirituals—two of my favorite musical genres—down in Texas during the first half of the twentieth century. He was part street preacher and part busker. His was a hard life. He was blinded as a child, possibly during a violent fight between his parents. When he was in his forties, his house burned down. Homeless, he slept in the ashy remains until he caught pneumonia. He was denied hospital treatment—possibly because he was black, perhaps because he was blind—and so died at the age of forty-eight.

Rev. Johnson's "What is the soul of a man?" tells of a quest to answer this vital question. His singing voice is graveled and husky, and he's accompanied by a woman, probably his wife. He asks various people for an answer. He reports visiting many countries to find out. He tells of speaking to doctors and lawyers but getting no satisfaction. Yet glimmers of light appear as he reads the Bible and ponders Jesus.

I'm still not ready to give a definitive answer to Johnson's vital question, but I am grateful for good company along the way. Gareth Brandt, a respected teacher and exemplary youth minister, is a reliable guide. One might even say—if you'll pardon the pun—a *men*tor to those of us still struggling with Johnson's quandary.

I identify with Brandt, a poetic dreamer who grew up among "real men." And I was touched by his tender explorations and humble confessions about his pilgrimage. His reflections on the Old Testament patriarch Joseph, someone whose wanderings are amply explored in Genesis, shed light on what we need to know as well.

I've read plenty of books on male spirituality by now, and this is one that I will remember well. It's been a long, long while since Blind Willie Johnson sang about his questing question. All vital issues, of course, generally need time for emerging clarity and discernment. What is the soul of a man, Reverend Johnson? Read this book and join the journey of discovery.

Arthur Paul Boers
Author of The Way is Made by Walking:
A Pilgrimage Along the Camino de Santiago

PREFACE

Men are famous—or infamous, as it may be—for being independent sorts. Strong men have traditionally or stereotypically been Lone Ranger types, fiercely independent and self-reliant. Jokes and stories abound about men who are hopelessly lost yet refuse to stop and ask for directions. "It must be around here somewhere," they grumble after the umpteenth time around the block. When men are injured, they often stoically grin and bear it, moving on to the next task or play. "I'll be fine," they say as they hobble along with a grimace that would make even the most cold-hearted mother respond with assistance. Why don't we ask for help? Why do we push on alone?

This book has been a communal project. A lot of people helped. But since I'm a typical man, it did not start out that way. My search for an understanding of men's spirituality began in a tangible way with a four-day retreat of complete silence and solitude on Vancouver Island at the beginning of my sabbatical from teaching. I was skeptical of the Christian men's movement, but I had never spent much time investigating what it was all about. I decided I needed to give it a chance.

During my retreat I began reading all the books on men's spirituality I could get my hands on, from perspectives including secular, Roman Catholic, mainline, and evangelical. I also read stories of men in the Bible. I wrote in my journal in response. I walked for miles along the beach, listening to the waves. My retreat of solitude and silence was a very valuable time for me, but all my reading left me deeply unsatisfied.

When men are injured, they often stoically grin and bear it, moving on to the next task or play. "I'll be fine," they say as they hobble along with a grimace that would make even the most cold-hearted mother respond with assistance.

I did not set out to write a book on men's spirituality. I set out on a personal quest. After reading more than a dozen books on the subject, I was left with the craving for another voice. And a voice inside said, "Then speak up!"

The thought of writing a book on men's spirituality terrified me because it seemed that I was just beginning this journey of discovery. But maybe this was a good way to start the journey—by writing about it. It didn't matter if anyone else ever read it.

Although I am an introvert and was invigorated by my retreat, after my time of solitude I was convinced that going solo was not the way to find a healthy and holistic male spirituality. This path must be traveled in company with other men: men of the Bible; my spiritual ancestors throughout history; and most importantly my friends, brothers, and colleagues.

I wondered about the possibility of discussing my writings with a small group of men, so I emailed a few dozen friends from church and colleagues at work. In less than twenty-four hours, I had a table full of men (and some on a waiting list!) who were interested in reading my writings and then meeting to talk about male spirituality one night a month.

I am grateful for each of the men in what came to be called the Mission Springs Group for their humor, seriousness, and authenticity in our monthly meetings during 2008: Phil Davis, John Dawson, Al Friesen, Tony Funk, Jon Nofziger, and Richard Thiessen. Thank you also to other colleagues and friends in Abbotsford who offered their own stories, critique, and counsel: Anne Andres, Walter Bergen, Janet Boldt, Bryan Born, Doug Epp, Jeff Nickel, Terry Penner, Michael Szuk, and Gay Lynn Voth.

In conversation, I began mentioning to other people what I was working on during my sabbatical and found an unexpected and enthusiastic interest in this men's spirituality project. Because of that, I thought I might increase the circle of conversation by starting a "virtual" group as well, so I contacted acquaintances across the continent. Again, within a very short time, about thirty people replied that they were interested in reading and responding to what I was writing.

As with any longitudinal project, the commitments sometimes wavered, but I appreciated all the responses and comments. Thanks to everyone who responded, especially Ken Penner, who was always the first to send in his articulate and insightful comments, and Dan and Julie Friesen, who were the only married couple to both respond on a regular basis.

A few other people need to be mentioned. Anne Campion saw a book in me nine years ago before it was even in my dreams. Byron Rempel-Burkholder was the first to believe that this project had something to contribute to a wider audience. My close friend Dennis Reimer kept me real and grounded. Ray Friesen has been a role model, advocate, and friend. My brother Glenn asked good questions, as he always does. My parents, Wilmer and Rosella Brandt, not only raised me toward spiritual manhood but also were supportive and interested in this project. My amazing wife, Cynthia, and our four children, Joel, Adriel, Sarina (thanks for the title), and Micah, know what kind of a man I really am and still love me and are proud of me. Amy Gingerich made the editorial process feel like we were on the same page. Thanks also to Mennonite Men for helping bring the manuscript to publication with financial support.

There's only one name on the cover, but I couldn't have written a book without the involvement of a lot of people. Like a stereotypical man, I drove around the block lost a few times, but I was also man enough to ask for directions. (The book may have started on a solitary retreat but it was completed in a busy family room in the midst of Lego™ building, dancing, homework, music playing and novel reading!)

In *Under Construction,* the first three chapters outline the quest for a constructive male spirituality: my personal journey in chapter 1; a summary and critical review of some of the literature in the field in chapter 2; and a search for a biblical story of a male who might become a mine of metaphors for us in chapter 3. Although Joseph is not the perfect man, or even a model man, his life story from birth to death is told in such detail that metaphors for men's spirituality abound.

The second section is an exploration of ten metaphors that come out of Joseph's story. Each chapter begins with one key word that names the metaphor *Each of your stories will be different from Joseph's, from mine, from other stories told in this book, but I hope you find here some fellow travelers in your quest to be a spiritual man.* and a paraphrase of part of Joseph's story. From this seed, each metaphor grows and branches out as we explore a contemporary spirituality for men.

I hope to tell a story of men's spirituality rather than give advice on how to be a good man or how to raise sons. Each of your stories will be different from Joseph's, from mine, from other stories told in this book, but I hope you find here some fellow travelers in your quest to be a spiritual man.

Gareth Brandt
October 25, 2009
In the family room at home

THE PERSONAL QUEST

What is a spiritual man?
A wild heart
running through the bush
beating primordial hairy chest
to claim his soul?

What is a spiritual man?
A cloistered monk
with bowed body,
closed eyes and
folded hands?

What is a spiritual man?
A phallic projection
erecting towers over,
ejecting power into
mother earth?

What is a spiritual man?
A chivalrous knight
killing his enemies,
protecting his clan
and his land?

What is a spiritual man?
I don't know
but I surely doubt
it is one of the above.

Can I be a real man and be authentically spiritual? Numerous authors, movements, and organizations have attempted to answer this question for us. Many of us have struggled alone because none of the ways suggested seem practical, biblical, or authentic to us. Yet the quest continues.

Many kinds of men are on this quest. Vic is a student at the college where I teach.[1] He grew up without an active father in his life. His parents divorced when he was in elementary school, and his mother has been in various relationships since then, so Vic has never had family stability or a consistent male role model. As a teenager, Vic found himself at a church youth group, and the youth pastor became a role model for him.

Vic is a sensitive, intuitive, creative young man who works part-time at an art store to get through college. He feels called to go into youth ministry so he can help young people who have had experiences similar to his own. Like many young men, Vic is in search of his unique spirituality and manhood. He has read a few books about how to be a good Christian man, but he says they made him feel like he was "not a real man" because he is not aggressive enough and doesn't really like outdoor activities or typical "guy movies" often used as illustrations. Vic is a "real man" and is deeply spiritual, but the current definitions of male spirituality have left him wondering and searching in vain.

Peter builds houses for a living. He is not a big-time contractor but a small-time laborer who works with his hands. He has been married for twenty years and has three children. Peter is a conscientious and diligent worker, and a sensitive and caring husband and father. But Peter thinks of himself as profoundly unspiritual. "I don't even know if I'm a Christian," I heard him say once. This surprised me, so I asked why he thought this way. "I don't do the things a Christian would do." He was referring to things like personal devotions, singing during worship services, and taking leadership in family Bible reading. He has heard that Christian men are supposed to lead in these kinds of things, and he feels he is a loser because his wife is more naturally gifted as a spiritual leader.

I wonder how many men are like Peter—men who I believe have a deep spirituality but are unaware of it because current definitions of male spirituality are so limited. These men don't fit the mold of the assertive, head-of-the-home, spiritual-leader type, so they whither away in the low self-esteem of apparent "unspirituality."

My story is different from Vic's or Peter's, but the struggle in the quest to be a spiritual man is the same.

I grew up in the 1960s in a rural prairie community. Both sides of my family had been farmers since they came to Canada to pioneer in the 1870s. A "real man" in my family was a farmer, carpenter, plumber, mechanic, or some kind of tradesman working with his hands, using brute strength and hard physical labor to make a living.

But I spent countless hours during my teenage years reading spiritual biographies and journaling out in the woods behind our farm yard. I dreamed. I wrote poetry. I was in touch with spiritual realities. As a university student, I enjoyed my summers working as a farm laborer, but I was not invigorated by the possibility of being a farmer or a tradesman for life. My adventure was a journey inward. Maybe I could at least grow up to be "spiritual," I thought, since it seemed impossible to be a "real man" according to the definitions around me.

Yet, like most boys, I wanted to grow up to be a man according to the values of the surrounding culture. I did a few things during my youth to express my masculinity. I played numerous sports with vigor, especially football and baseball, and I was pretty good at them. I loved competition and the feeling of running full tilt in an open field. I rebelled against the church, because church was for sissies. Because of my intuition and romantic nature, I could also express my manliness through relationships with girls. I had many girl-friends during adolescence and young adulthood. But many of those relationships ended as "just friends," prob-ably because the girls wanted the jock as a boyfriend, not the guy who recited poetry.

I wanted to grow up to be a man according to the values of the surrounding culture.

I studied psychology in university—a field dominated by females. I'm sure the engineering department's gender statistics were the other way around. In studying psychol-ogy, I was invigorated by other students, mostly women, who knew how to articulate their feelings and get beyond surface things. One young woman I met there—the one I eventually married—appreciated my openness and sensi-tivity to her. Yet I was initially attracted to her because she knew how to throw a football!

Defining *Spirituality*

In later years of theological studies, I began to define and describe the elusive concept of spirituality. Spirituality is the quest for relation to the Other.[2] To be spiritual is to be in touch with the self, with God, and with others. Many variables influence our spirituality: age, culture, personality, gender. As Franciscan priest Richard Rohr writes, "Spirituality is a matter of having a source of energy within which is a motivating and directing force for living."[3] This means that spirituality includes all of life, not only activities such as prayer, meditation, and worship. Spirituality, then, is how we express our faith in God through these activities but also through our work, play, daily routines, and primarily through our relationships.

Spirituality is the quest for relation to the Other. To be spiritual is to be in touch with the self, with God, and with others.

In my graduate studies, newly discovered feminine metaphors for God in the Bible enriched my soul. Even my first spiritual director was a woman. I think my unconscious conclusion was that men are unspiritual, so how could I benefit from a male spiritual director? In university and seminary studies, I developed a strong connection to feminine spirituality. I guess you could say I discovered my "feminine side," and this helped me to become a more whole, spiritual human being.

A few weeks ago I participated in a spiritual pilgrimage with a group of adults from across North America. A majority of the pilgrims were involved in ministry of some kind, but the most notable demographic was this: the women outnumbered the men seven to one. Why? We three men discussed this at the back of the bus. ("Men have to be near the engine," one of them joked, even though none of us knew much about engines.) We agreed that generally women are more in touch with their spiritual center and thus are more likely to be interested in an experiential course on communal spirituality. We wondered if one of the reasons men weren't interested was because an appropriate spirituality for men had never been articulated for them. Yet I believe that spirituality is not only for pastors, monks, and those involved in various men's movements. All men can be deeply spiritual.

Spirituality is not only for pastors, monks, and those involved in various men's movements. All men can be deeply spiritual.

Men and women express their spirituality differently. Most people would acknowledge that women are generally more spiritually attuned than men and more in touch with their inner selves and emotions. The feminist movement also has helped bring energy and validity to a unique feminine spirituality. In contrast, men tend to be more left-brained and rational, muscular and physical. "Real" men, it seems, are not spiritual. Various authors have lamented that the only spiritual man in church is the pastor or priest, and the rest of spirituality has been feminine or "a kind of 'neuter' religion."[4] Thus men are left without a spirituality and don't enjoy church (which we could call a communal expression of spirituality). Yet there is definitely such a thing as male spirituality. So what is it like?

In Search of a Uniquely Male Spirituality

In midlife I began to hunger for something more than what I had gleaned through formal studies. I began to think specifically about my unique spirituality as a man. In my teaching, I have always emphasized the importance of personal or human spiritual qualities, and I believed that many so-called gender differences in spirituality were primarily culturally produced. I also believed that personality and culture had a lot more to do with shaping spirituality than gender.

Yet if women were claiming that there was a unique female spirituality, then there must also be a unique male spirituality. But what is it like?

I am a man. My spirituality is not a separate compartment that allows me to be feminine in that area and masculine in other areas. My spirituality is holistic; it is about who I am—all of who I am, not a specialized and separate compartment somewhere. What does it mean to be a real spiritual man? What is male spirituality like?[5]

I did not find a lot of answers when I asked this question of men in my circle of family, friends, colleagues, and students. Even those who were experienced readers and men's convention-goers seemed to be in the same rudderless boat. Young men, in particular, whom I interact with at the college where I teach, were asking the question, even if not articulating it clearly or overtly. This told me that men are yearning for an alternative voice in male spirituality. They have not yet found what they are looking for.

My personal quest begins without a notion of where it is going. I do not come with years of experience as a men's speaker or as a participant in a men's organization. I have no formula that I have tested in years of ministry. This is not a how-to book, because I am on the journey of finding out how to be a spiritual man. I come with nothing to offer but my own story and the stories of my friends, and an academic background driven in part by my personal predicament.

Writing about spirituality is like being soul-naked in front of the mirror and not knowing who else is watching. I speak from that place in my heart where I am most myself.[6]

My quest begins and ends with a question: what is a spiritual man? Someday, and possibly through this writing exercise, I will live into the answer. Perhaps men's spirituality is more about living the question than finding the answer.

This quest is not only an individual one for each man and not only for men as a collective. It is part of the larger human quest for relation to the Transcendent and for peaceful coexistence and mutual thriving as a human race, as an entire creation. Frankly, men's self-understanding is significant in the outworking of God's salvation in the world. Men, and in particular Christian men, have been a big part of the problem over the centuries, so we must be part of the solution for the future.

My quest begins and ends with a question: what is a spiritual man?. . . Perhaps men's spirituality is more about living the question than finding the answer.

As I begin, I feel akin to Richard Rohr in the personal opening to his book on male initiation. He writes,

> Men like me, with access to all manner of privilege and freedom not granted to others, must talk

about the male game from within. I think you can only unlock spiritual things from within. Paralleling what women are saying about themselves, men must first and finally interpret men. Surely for the last twenty years, and maybe for much of history, we have largely been interpreted by whatever power group was in charge—doing none of us much good—and very recently by women, which has been both good and bad for us. Men have not, however, described their own souls very well, as they did not have the language or even the interest.[7]

It is my purpose to contribute to the articulation of the male soul. Like the men described by Rohr, I may not do it very well, but my hope is that this book offers a different perspective from what is already out there.

What is a spiritual man? Join me in living the question. Let's journey together in this quest.

THE QUEST IN LITERATURE

Conscious articulation of gender differences in spirituality seems to be a modern invention. There have been numerous spiritual writings by both men and women throughout the history of the church, but very few attempts to label a spiritual writing as applying only to men or only to women. Most of the writers seem to assume that they are writing for all people, female and male.

However, it is interesting to compare two spiritual classics that have endured the test of time: *Pilgrim's Progress* by John Bunyan, and Teresa of Avila's *Interior Castle*. Although these were written a century apart (*Pilgrim's Progress* dates from the 1670s, *Interior Castle* from the 1570s) and from different theological persuasions, it is noteworthy that the male writer uses the upward journey motif while the female writer explores the various interior rooms of a mansion. If we read these two ancient writings as if they were meant to reflect gender-specific spiritualities, we immediately see a significant difference. Although both the journey and the

There have been numerous spiritual writings by both men and women throughout the history of the church, but very few attempts to label a spiritual writing as applying only to men or only to women.

home motifs are valuable for men and women, I primarily use the journey metaphor to develop a specifically male spirituality.

Modern Literature

The modern "men's movement" in both secular and Christian circles has sought to answer the question, what is a spiritual man? So a survey of literature necessarily focuses on recent writings in the area of male spirituality. Robert Bly's *Iron John* and Sam Keen's *Fire in the Belly* attempt to do this for secular or unaffiliated men. For Christians, Roman Catholic priest Richard Rohr's book *The Wild Man's Journey* and most recently John Eldredge's *Wild at Heart* have been most influential. A spate of similar literature has accompanied these more well-known titles. The Promise Keepers organization also has tried to define men's spirituality through literature, mass rallies, and various educational gatherings. Although coming from vastly different theological and spiritual backgrounds, all these sources use surprisingly similar images and metaphors.

Male Archetypes

Four basic archetypes of male spirituality are utilized by the modern men's movement in various ways and with a variety of vocabularies. Webster's defines an archetype as "the original pattern or model of all things in that type." Therefore, archetypes for male spirituality are models that represent the deep desires within us that are filled with generative power.[1]

Psychologists Robert Moore and Douglas Gillette were

among the first modern writers to delineate the four basic masculine archetypes: king, warrior, lover, and magician.[2] They describe these archetypes as blueprints that are foundational to how men think, feel, and behave. The following brief descriptions are composites combining the vocabulary of various authors.

The first archetype is the *king*. The king, or father, symbolizes security, generativity, protection, and strong leadership. The king is the father figure who reproduces, provides, reigns, and gives order to family, community, and country.

The king is the father of the second archetype: the *warrior*, knight, soldier, or adventurer. A warrior is called to conquer and is portrayed as young, energetic, and wild. He has pledged allegiance to the king and/or to a cause, and he is

A warrior is called to conquer and is portrayed as young, energetic, and wild.

itching for a battle to fight. The warrior is characterized by courage and disciplined aggression; he protects and "fights for" those put under his care.

The third archetype is the *lover*, poet, musician, or minstrel. The lover is the sexual man who woos and feels and is passionate. The lover is the emotional friend who connects with others in the world, particularly women.

The final archetype is the *magician*, sage, or prophet. Writers who are uncomfortable with mystical language prefer the terms *mentor* or *teacher*. The magician is the wise man or elder who passes on the values of manhood to the next generation.

Various writers on men's spirituality claim that these archetypes are as old as time, and that every boy throughout history and in the present aspires to these archetypes deep in his heart. These claims are backed by selected theological, historical, anthropological, and psychological sources. Even though men obviously don't become these archetypes literally, they become them—or yearn to become them—spiritually.

Each writer who uses these archetypes interprets and describes them in his own way, but each gives examples of how the archetypes are innate in every boy and man. Their examples often point to boyhood—for instance, suggesting that aggressive games like "Cowboys and Indians" are instinctive to the male child's soul. Writers' archetypal examples also come from history and from certain types of movies and literature that all men supposedly enjoy. These movies usually involve intense action and violent resolutions.

Sometimes the archetypes are chronological and developmental.[3] For example, a young warrior leaves home on an adventure to conquer foreign lands for his king. After the warrior has fought off the evil hordes guarding the castle, he is declared a man. He goes on to find the damsel in distress hidden and helpless in a dark corner. Smitten, he rescues her from a life of incompleteness and loneliness. As they bear children, the man raises his sons to be warriors. In middle age, he becomes the king of his realm. And, of course, they live happily ever after. Finally, in old age, the man becomes the wise sage who passes on the legacy of manhood to the next generation. This is a simplified caricature, but it is definitely present in literature on male spirituality.

Thankfully, authors do acknowledge, to varying degrees, that there is a dark side of each archetype and that each can be twisted to give assent to violence, domination, abuse, and various addictions. They warn of the dangers of improper balance in living them,[4] but they all seem to assume that these archetypes are universal to all men.

Questioning the Warrior

These archetypes have some validity, and I relate to aspects of them. Numerous friends have said they see me as a warrior of sorts, even in the writing of this book. I also played sports with aggression and energy as a young man, and I see life as an adventure to live passionately. Complacency is a most dreaded disease to me! My vocation is to be a teacher and mentor, the biblical prophets inspire me, and at heart I am a poet. So I do not dismiss the archetypes as having no value for a Christian male spirituality, but they leave me unsatisfied. Are there other archetypes, models, motifs, and metaphors that might also be relevant?

I do not dismiss the archetypes as having no value for a Christian male spirituality, but they leave me unsatisfied.

There also seem to be inherent problems with each of these four archetypes. Where do these archetypes come from? Christian authors often use the Bible as a source of texts and illustrations, but not as the primary well for the archetypes. The claim is that these archetypes are as old as time, but the terms and much of the imagery come from the medieval era in western Europe, an era dominated by the feudal system. The idyllic setting is a battlefield in a forested wilderness, and the dominant model of manhood is the honorable crusading knight.

Is the bloody and brutal era of the Crusades a good one on which to base our idea of Christian male spirituality? Certainly the medieval era was not the golden age of human civilization in Europe. It definitely was the golden age of male supremacy, but not the best example of a holistic male spirituality. If male spirituality is based on the medieval king and warrior, it is a spirituality that is paranoid in its quest to hang on to power and to conquer whoever might be labeled the enemy.

I fear that too much of the present evangelical male spirituality movement is indeed based on this paranoia, under the guise of biblical manhood. This might be part of the reason war and male dominance persist in our culture. If this is manhood, then feminists are right in saying that men are to blame for the problems in our world. But is this Christian manhood?

Counselor and evangelical author John Eldredge uses warrior/adventurer imagery and redefines the lover as the rescuer. Eldredge says that every man has three desires deep within him: (1) to be in a battle, (2) to be on an adventure, (3) to rescue a beauty.[5] How has Eldredge determined this? He has found these desires deep within his own heart; has talked to many men; has read books and watched movies; and has found this true because of his belief that God has these characteristics and that men are made in the image of God. Is Eldredge merely extrapolating his particular strand of masculinity onto the rest of us? His conclusion leaves me wondering whether his is a testosterone-laced version of manhood based on the gospel of Mel Gibson[6] as much as on the gospel of Jesus Christ.

The Promise Keepers' vision of manhood also emphasizes warrior imagery, and it has had an impressive influence on the lives of North American men in the past few decades.[7] A friend of mine, who was raised on Promise Keepers rallies since he was a teenager and has gone to many events, says that the warrior motif has been a mainstay at Promise Keepers events, although it has grown stronger since 9/11. "Whereas before the war I can remember things like doing a Maori dance to express the male warrior spirituality," he said, "after the war began, everything became a battle. We were told that as men we are in this 'war that we need to win at all costs.' It seemed like there was nothing more manly than a guy in a military uniform."

I know of a church where, after finishing a Christian men's course, the men had a knighting ceremony, complete with medieval swords, as part of the Sunday worship service. Although the warrior imagery is spiritualized, many illustrations of this type of male spirituality are military heroes in bloody battle.

The warrior archetype addresses what is seen as the primary problem for men: we are too passive and nice. The lament is that the typical North American man stands in an assembly line or sits in a cubicle all week; when he comes home, all he does is sit on the couch, watch television, and drink beer. The evangelical version just omits the beer and adds church attendance. Characters Bart Simpson and Ned Flanders of "The Simpsons" embody these caricatures. If they are our models of manhood, then we are to be pitied indeed! But are men really that bad? Are we just a bunch of passive couch potatoes in need of a kick in the pants? And is idolizing warriors the best way to address the problem of passivity?

This renewed emphasis on a tougher, wilder masculine spirituality is a reaction to what evangelical men's leaders see as a capitulation to feminism. They believe that this capitulation is one of the reasons the church in the West is floundering. Mark Driscoll, one of the most outspoken leaders of this movement, says,

> There is a strong drift toward the hard theological left. Some emergent types [want] to recast Jesus as a limp-wrist hippie in a dress with a lot of product in His hair, who drank decaf and made pithy Zen statements about life while shopping for the perfect pair of shoes. In Revelation, Jesus is a prize fighter with a tattoo down His leg, a sword in His hand and the commitment to make someone bleed. That is a guy I can worship. I cannot worship the hippie, diaper, halo Christ because I cannot worship a guy I can beat up.[8]

I would not want to worship either one of these caricatures of Jesus, and I am not sure either of them is particularly biblical. Yet Driscoll's quote illustrates the nature of the wild warrior male spirituality prevalent in so much of the literature today.

According to much of the recent material coming out of the evangelical men's movement, for men to regain their rightful male spirituality, they need to recover their strength, aggression, authority, leadership, wildness, ruggedness, fighting spirit, toughness, assertiveness, and so on. Paul Coughlin, author of *No More Christian Nice Guy*, says that Christian men need to stop being so emotionless, passive, and polite, like "gentle Jesus meek and mild."[9] Instead of being a "nice guy," they should become "good men" who are passionate, protective, and proactive—men who stand up for themselves and the women and children under their headship.

Coughlin argues that no woman is attracted to a passive man, and no nice guy ever got a promotion or gained a medal of military valor. The implication is that catching a woman and "winning" at work or on the battlefield are the marks of a real man. I am all for getting up off the couch, but there are other metaphors that help us

For men to regain their rightful male spirituality, they need to recover their strength, aggression, authority, leadership, wildness, ruggedness, fighting spirit, toughness, assertiveness, and so on.

define a "good man" or a "real spiritual man"—metaphors that do not call us to conquer and dominate.

As a pacifist,[10] I have always found warrior imagery troublesome, but that in itself does not discount its validity. Spiritual warfare and warriors are biblical concepts, but they have been mistranslated into dominance and violence in both North America and around the world. The Crusades, the "war on terror," and the rampant abuse of women in their own homes are some extreme examples. But men are not born to kill and conquer; they must be taught and desensitized—and even dehumanized—for them to be able to succeed at war.[11]

While some men have found this metaphor encouraging, I think the warrior metaphor must be used cautiously. Personally, I do not find the warrior at all helpful for developing a relevant and constructive male spirituality in an age of increasing terror and violence. Surely men can be spiritually adventurous and courageous without becoming dominant and violent.

Seeking Alternatives

Three archetypes outlined in this chapter are based on prominent leaders in society: kings, warriors, and wise men. Yet these three archetypes represent only a small minority of men. The lover often is portrayed as a court jester or entertainer, which also describes only a minority. Where are the archetypes for common men? Is manhood really just about aspiring to conquer and rule and repeat the cycle? Is male spirituality primarily one of dissatisfaction with one's lot in life and a constant aspiration for a higher rank?

Three archetypes outlined in this chapter are based on prominent leaders in society: kings, warriors, and wise men. Yet these three archetypes represent only a small minority of men.

What about the peasant-farmers and the craftsmen who have made up the majority of the male population throughout history? Is there not an adventure in the rhythm of the seasons, of planting and nurturing and harvest, of herding and caring for livestock? Is there not fulfillment in the construction of a house, the completion of a project, the accomplishment of a communal task? Did my Mennonite ancestors dream of being warriors and adventurers, longing to leave the drudgery and daily grind of their domestic life to go sail some seas, kill some enemies, and rescue a fair maiden? Maybe some did. But I believe most of them were invigorated by their life and content with their lot.

The dangers and shortcomings of the popular archetypes cause us to seek others—archetypes more conducive to giving witness to God's work in the building of a peaceful world. Jesus came to inaugurate a commonwealth of love and justice where boundaries and hierarchies, dominance and violence will be no more (see Luke 4:16-21). A spirituality for men is not only about self-actualization and fulfillment; it is also about salvation for humanity and the planet. Men have taken part in ruining creation, and now men need to repent and participate in God's redemption of the world. The future of our race and planet is at least partly dependent on how men answer their identity question. How can we be uniquely and authentically men and partner equally with women in the creative and redemptive mission that the archetypal human being, Jesus Christ, started for us?

The archetypal approaches to masculine spirituality have inspired and encouraged many men. But there are men like me who want to be men and want to be spiritual men, yet none of the models have sufficiently helped in our journey. These archetypes have the tendency to view male spirituality as dominant and conquest-minded to the neglect of a male spirituality that is more constructive and nurturing. Richard Rohr obviously began to realize this need in the rewriting of his earlier book, *The Wild Man's Journey*, which is now entitled *From Wild Man to Wise*

The archetypal approaches to masculine spirituality have inspired and encouraged many men. But there are men like me who want to be men and want to be spiritual men, yet none of the models have sufficiently helped in our journey.

Man. Maybe all men need to be challenged to move beyond the wild warrior archetype for the good of our society.

Metaphors, Not Archetypes

In fact, maybe we need to let go of the archetypes altogether. An archetype is a strong, almost coercive concept in and of itself. I am always skeptical of people who claim, "This is the one" or "Here is the model for everyone."

Obviously all men might share some common spiritual characteristics, but each man is also different from all others. Therefore, a variety of metaphors would serve our purposes more effectively than an archetype.

Archetypes tend to make large universal claims applicable to all men everywhere. My aim here is more modest: to present some biblical metaphors of male spirituality as alternatives to the dominant archetypes that have been put forth. Obviously all men might share some common spiritual characteristics, but each man is also different from all others. Therefore, a variety of metaphors would serve our purposes more effectively than an archetype.

Although metaphors do not make the universal claims of an archetype, they do have transformative power in combination with the work of the Spirit. A metaphor is a symbol, picture, or figurative expression of a deeper reality. Images and symbols are very important in spirituality, and all religions have a long history of using symbols to express spiritual realities.

It is the Spirit of God who transforms us, but metaphors help us get beneath the surface (where transformation happens) of our conscious life to the place where we have put up roadblocks to meaningful change. Songs and poems—in fact, all art forms—use metaphors that awaken spiritual realities. Metaphors have a way of sneaking under our skin to where the depth of the spirit waits to be touched and transformed. What biblical metaphors might transform men toward the purposes of God in this world?

THE BIBLICAL QUEST

As a Christ-follower, it is important for me that the metaphors, models, and motifs for male spirituality come from the authorities and traditions of my life. For me, the Bible is the revelation of God's story and God's person; it's an authority and guide in my life. This leads me to wonder: what models of men's spirituality are there for followers of Jesus who use the Bible as a guide for life? Let's search the Bible for a man's story, a narrative that provides some metaphors for developing a constructive men's spirituality.

God

A number of authors build their models on God's wildness and on the wild and rugged character of Jesus, the incarnation of God. Although it may make logical sense to use God or Jesus as a model, doing so makes it very easy to create God in the image of a particular type of man or to create Jesus in our own image.[1]

Most male writers acknowledge that God also has a feminine nature, because women too are made in the image of God (see Genesis 1:27). It seems to me that this is the reason we cannot use only God or Jesus as a model for male spirituality: God is both masculine and feminine. God may be wild and undomesticated, but that should then be a characteristic of human spirituality and not only of male spirituality.

We cannot use God as a distinctly male model of spirituality because the ways we determine which characteristics are male or female are based on criteria we bring in from the outside, meaning our own experiences of men and women. God is female and male; that's why when God created humans in the divine image, God created them male and female. The two genders are part of the diversity of God. Having either a penis or a vagina defines one's biological identity as male or female but it does not define one's spirituality. Obviously, since God does not have a penis and a vagina, being created in the image of God goes deeper than our different sex organs. There must be something in the soul that is masculine and feminine. The criteria then for a unique male spirituality must come from outside what God is like, since God is both masculine and feminine, and it must come from outside Jesus, since Jesus gives us a model for what all humans are to be like.

> *We cannot use God as a distinctly male model of spirituality because the ways we determine which characteristics are male or female are based on criteria we bring in from the outside.*

All our descriptions of God are necessarily and admittedly limited and anthropomorphic. God's character both transcends and includes the nature of both genders. One of the most intriguing recent descriptions of God that includes both genders is found in William P. Young's novel, *The Shack*.[2] Young does not purport to explore men's spirituality, but his book does so profoundly.

The main character, Mackenzie Phillips, wrestles with the nature of God in light of personal tragedy and loss. God comes to him first of all as Abba, pictured as a robust African-American woman who cooks up various culinary delights. The Trinity is rounded out by her son, Jesus, a rather homely Palestinian man who works in the woodshop, and the Holy Spirit, an elusive and mysterious Asian woman who favors the garden as her place of creativity. Sophia, as Wisdom, even makes an appearance as a thoughtful, Hispanic, female judge.

Part of seeking a holistic male spirituality might be a renewed appreciation for God as father, especially in relation to how we view our earthly fathers. But it also means knowing God as mother. Depending on the man, that might be just as important in the development of his spirituality.

Jesus

I believe that the historical Jesus was a man who walked the dusty roads of Palestine in the first century. He was not half man and half woman; he had a penis and a beard. However, I do not believe that Jesus' gender is significant as a revelation of what God is like. Jesus did not primarily become a male; he became a human being. The incarnation is about God becoming human, not about God becoming a human male.

If we use Jesus as a model for male spirituality, we must also use him as a model for female spirituality. Jesus came to save both women and men, and to show all people how to be spiritual. Jesus is an archetype for all humanity, not specifically for men in any way. Saying Jesus is a model only for men is like saying Jesus is a model only for Jews and no other group.

There is an infinite storehouse of Jesus-spirituality. This spirituality is what being a follower of Jesus is all about. The discovery of it is for men and women, Jews and Gentiles, and all people of the earth. A male spirituality should definitely be consistent with the character and story of Jesus. In contrast, some of the archetypes and literary descriptions mentioned previously are not consistent with Jesus. A male spirituality should reflect the character of Christ, but so should a female spirituality.

Adam

From a biblical standpoint, only Adam would suffice as an "original model." Although Philip Culbertson, a scholar in practical theology, entitles his book *New Adam*, he does not use Adam as an archetype.[3] In fact, Culbertson begins the book by pointing out that all people begin as females. It is only at about six or seven weeks after conception that the presence of the Y chromosome switches some fetuses from female to male. In that sense, Genesis 2 has it backward, according to Culbertson; Eve produced Adam, rather than the other way around.[4]

It is not necessary to get into biological determinism and all its controversial implications here. The point is this that, although Adam (literally "earthling") was an archetype in a way, he is not particularly useful as a metaphor for male spirituality. We know very little about him as a person outside the creation story, which is primarily a theological explanation of origins.

The Bible is full of other men we might consider as models of male spirituality. I did an informal survey asking the question, "Who's your favorite Bible man?" There were almost as many men in the Bible mentioned as there were responders. This tells me that there is no one man in the Bible who can provide a model to capture all of male spirituality.

My search, then, was to find the story of one man in the Bible who might give us a variety of metaphors for male spirituality. Because there is no

The Bible is full of other men we might consider as models of male spirituality.

ideal spiritual man in the Bible, I looked for one man's story that provides us with some metaphors for being a spiritual man in the twenty-first century. Let's explore the spirituality of a few men of the Bible as we search for a metaphorical story.

Paul

The first biblical character that came to mind was Paul. He is, after all, the author of more than half the New Testament. I've never particularly liked Paul. I'm not sure why. Maybe it's the way he has been interpreted in the past, particularly as negative toward women. For example, Paul does not allow women to speak in church (see 1 Corinthians 14:34-35); they must always be under the authority of men (see 1 Corinthians 11:5-6). Of course, these texts have to be taken in their historical and cultural context. And Pauline texts that point to the equality and mutual submission of men and women, such as Galatians 3:28 and Ephesians 5:21, must also be considered.

No one knows conclusively that Paul was single, but he lauds the single life as ideal for a dynamic spirituality (see 1 Corinthians 7). In some ways it might be easier to develop a male spirituality for celibate men. In the history of the church, celibate men such as monks have been held up as role models of male spirituality. The spiritual writers and mystics of antiquity, and even of the modern era, have often been celibate men (from Saint Francis to Thomas Merton). Sexuality and spirituality are so intertwined that being in a sexually active relationship just makes an active spirituality more complex. Yet it would be nice to have a male spirituality that would be positive for married men as well as single men.

We know a lot of Paul's opinions on things and his teachings, but we do not know much about Paul the man, because he didn't write much about his personal life. This seems essential if we are to develop metaphors for real-life spirituality from Paul's life.

John the Baptist

Author Richard Rohr also mentions John the Baptist,[5] who is obviously the quintessential "wild man" and thus a good one to use when developing a spiritual metaphor for men. I've often identified with John in my eccentric, raging prophetic moments. He was not afraid to be unique, to be his own kind of man. But John was a loner called to live on the fringes of society. Most of us are called to a male spirituality in the midst of a life of interaction with people: wives, children, co-workers, and neighbors.

Peter and the Twelve

Peter is the disciple we get to know best. One of my given names is Peter, and I've always been intrigued by his strong, forthright, passionate nature. There are parts of his life many men can relate to: impulsiveness (see Mark 9:5), intuitive insights (see 8:29), failure (see 14:66-72); readiness to protect (see Luke 22:49-50); and taking charge (see Acts 2:14). Unfortunately, again we must acknowledge that we really know very little about Peter's personal life from the Gospels. His persona has become so wrapped up in his being the rock and the foundation that it is difficult to get to know the man himself.

What about the other eleven? John is too elusive; we do not have enough narrative to go on. Many can identify with the doubts of Thomas, but again we know very little about his life or person. Judas might embody some of our greed and self-interest. But, really, no disciple serves us as a metaphor of male spirituality.

David

The most obvious Old Testament character of choice is David, the ancestor of Jesus. Unlike the stories of men in the New Testament, David's story includes extensive narrative. Even the psalms he wrote reveal some of his character or are linked to events in his life.

I am surprised that David is not used more by the warrior spirituality writers—he was a warrior, after all. David killed Goliath when he was only a youth and went on to kill tens of thousands in battle. He was always my favorite Bible character as a boy. I'm not sure what I liked about him most. Was it that he was an underdog who defeated the giant; a warrior the women swooned over; a loyal friend to Jonathan; a skilled musician; an emotional and passionate poet? Eugene Peterson has written a brilliant book about David's spirituality, although not in terms of a specifically male spirituality.[6]

David probably exemplifies the four archetypes the best of any biblical man, although not necessarily in a positive way. Not only was he a valiant warrior and hot-blooded lover, he was also an obedient shepherd boy, an emotional poet, and a man who actually had a close male friend.

Yet David did not grow old gracefully. His kingdom fell apart from the inside. His family was wrecked by the problems created by his own sins. These sins brought David and some of his sons to the grave.

All men have sinned, and far too many in our society of fractured relationships can identify with David's sin of adultery. While this story illustrates the pain that David's sins caused for him and his family, I'm not sure we want to hold up David as a model. I don't want some perfect, sinless man either, because he would seem unreal and impossible to relate to. I do want someone who wrestled with life and won out, so to speak.

All men have sinned, and far too many in our society of fractured relationships can identify with David's sin of adultery. While this story illustrates the pain that David's sins caused for him and his family, I'm not sure we want to hold up David as a model.

The Patriarchs

What about one of the patriarchs? First, patriarchy has a negative vibe in contemporary western society. Abraham was the father of many nations, which included not only Jews but also all the other nations in the Middle East. If we talk spiritually, this includes all the nations of the world. But

Abraham's culture was so different from ours—with polygamy, human sacrifice, and marriage to close relatives all seen as acceptable—that it makes him hard for us to relate to. Jacob and Esau could exemplify the two sides of masculinity, but neither of them is likable—Esau as the reckless macho warrior and Jacob as the conniving, paranoid, self-centered mama's boy.

Moses

The story of Moses provides another extensive personal narrative, and the first five books of the Bible are ascribed to him. We have a variety of stories about Moses' life: his birth, his leadership of the Hebrew people as they left Egypt and wandered in the wilderness, his death at Mount Nebo. This makes Moses a favorite when it comes to making movies, but his real persona gets mixed up with the various ways he is portrayed on screen.

Moses' life provides some good metaphors: protection as a child, dealing with sin, a unique calling from God, and his many adventures in leading Israel. Along with Abraham and David, Moses is a primary leader in Jewish history. Yet this is not advantageous when searching for metaphors for ordinary, modern men.

Judges, Prophets, and Others

The list of male leaders in the nation of Israel is almost endless. We could explore Joshua and subsequent judges, such as Gideon and Samson. They make particularly good models of warriors, but I have already outlined the problems with warriors as models of male spirituality.

None of the prophets work as models either, again

because of a lack of personal details and life narrative. Although I've always liked Jeremiah because I can identify with his melancholy personality, self-doubt, and yet confident proclamation, there just isn't enough narrative available.

The story of Jonah is intriguing, but there isn't much archetypal, exemplary, or metaphorical material. Daniel has some possibilities. His story includes: leaving home, loyalty to faith and values, enduring danger, close male friends, rising through the ranks of power, prophetic pronouncements, and so on. The problem is that we know very little about Daniel's family life, where he came from, and what he was like as an older adult.

I'm getting weary of listing the multitude of men in the Bible. I've even thought along the way that it would be good to consider *all* the men in the Bible as our community of spiritual wanderers. But that would be far too complex.

Is there a story of one biblical man who might provide us with a multiplicity of metaphors for male spirituality?

Is there a story of one biblical man who might provide us with a multiplicity of metaphors for male spirituality?

I had a dream that revealed it should be Joseph. How can I argue with a dream?

Joseph

Why is Joseph's story a good pick as a metaphor of male spirituality? First, there is a lot of good narrative about his

life: birth and boyhood, young adulthood, family relationships, adventures, career, prison, moving, climbing up the
corporate ladder. This story has it all! Some might say that
Joseph is too squeaky clean, that he doesn't have any notice-
able failures. But most of us
identify more with Joseph's
internal struggles of pride
and revenge than with

Joseph is a real person with a real life that many of us can identify with.

Moses' murder or David's adultery. Joseph is a real person
with a real life that many of us can identify with. Although
Joseph's life does not have a wonderfully dramatic end, it
does end well.

Different incidents in Joseph's life—stories ranging
from his birth to his death and many experiences in
between—make good metaphors for a developmental
view of male spirituality. The spirituality symbolized by the
metaphors may be experienced in any order and added to
each other at any point. One's spirituality does not need
to develop in an orderly fashion, going from one stage
and moving on to the next only when the previous stage
is complete. Some men experience them sequentially as
they mature; others do not.

Similarly, some metaphors from Joseph's life may be
meaningful for certain men but not for others. The important thing is that we continue to process our experiences
and thus add to our storehouse of memories and
metaphors that nurture us toward wholeness. Faith develops, even if the process is not neat or orderly, but full of
twists and turns. Joseph's life is a good example of this.

My use of the Joseph character and story is more alle-
gorical than exegetical.[7] My reflection does not claim any

special interpretive authority or insight into the original author's intent. My desire is simply to mine the story of a biblical man for some metaphors of men's spirituality. Walter Brueggemann writes that, although metaphors are "concrete words rooted in visible reality, they are

Faith develops, even if the process is not neat or orderly, but full of twists and turns. Joseph's life is a good example of this.

also enormously elastic, giving full play to imagination in stretching and extending far beyond the concrete referent to touch all kinds of experience."[8]

Joseph's story provides ten metaphors that I will flesh out and expand through the stories of other biblical men, a theology centered on Jesus, my own story, and the stories of my friends and acquaintances.

Each chapter in the following section begins with a loose paraphrase of part of the Joseph narrative. Read the story and meditate on the metaphor. Then read the rest of the chapter. Each metaphor will travel in various directions from its beginning in the Joseph story. Each explores various aspects of contemporary male spirituality that are not necessarily inherent in the biblical story of Joseph, but Joseph's story gives seeds from which they grow and branch out.[9]

4

BELOVED

God remembered Rachel and heard her prayers for
a child. She became pregnant and had a son.
Rachel said, "God has taken away my disgrace at
not having children." She named him Joseph,
which means "add," praying, "May God add yet
another son to me."

After Rachel had given birth to Joseph, Jacob
packed up his twelve children, his wives and servants, and moved back to where he had grown
up. Rachel gave birth to another son on the way
back, but she died as a result of the difficult labor.
Joseph grew up without a mother.

Jacob's family settled where his father, Isaac,
had lived in the land of Canaan. Jacob loved
Joseph dearly because he was the child of Rachel,
whom he loved, and was born to him in his old
age. To show Joseph his love, Jacob made him an
elaborately embroidered colorful coat and gave it
to him as a gift. It was obvious to everyone that
Jacob loved Joseph more than anyone else in the
family, and this made Joseph's brothers angry and
they grew to hate him. They wouldn't even talk to
him. (Genesis 30:22-24; 35:16-19; 37:1-4;
author's retelling)

To know that we are beloved by our father and our Father—what a great place from which to begin the journey of male spirituality!

Joseph is his father Jacob's favorite son. This favoritism has always bothered me, and it obviously bothered his jealous brothers, but we do not need to get hung up with that detail here. Whatever Jacob's motives were, Joseph knew that he was a special son. He knew that he was deeply loved. I'm sure Jacob's other sons yearned to be loved as Joseph was loved.

To know that we are beloved by our father and our Father—what a great place from which to begin the journey of male spirituality!

Joseph's multicolored coat symbolizes this specialness. This sense of being the "beloved" becomes the foundation for the rest of his journey. It is not hard to imagine that it was this love that enabled Joseph to endure slavery and separation. This love kept him grounded when he was tempted and became outwardly successful.

Love

The experiential knowledge that we are deeply and unconditionally loved is at the core of male spirituality. To be loved is the grounding of all human spirituality, but it is particularly poignant for men. It becomes the center point for all our experimentation and exploration. Richard Rohr writes, "If [we] are tethered at some centre point, it is amazing how far out [we] can fly and not get lost. . . . If we know our original blessing, we can easily handle our original sin."[1] We may struggle, we may fall into sin, we may experience rejection, but we can always come back to this basis of our spirituality. Being the beloved is the original blessing that grounds the spirituality of men.

Love is often associated with sentimentality and "warm fuzzies," and therefore the whole concept of loving and being loved is often difficult for men. Male love is seen as initiating, protecting, and defending. While that is appropriate, what about receiving love? That might be the most difficult part—and the most important part—in the development of a healthy male spirituality.

Being "beloved" is often associated with female receptivity. For example, in the Song of Songs, the male is the lover and the "beloved" is the female. Yet to know and experience being loved is profound and deep. A man is incapable of loving until he has experienced being loved.

Some men sexualize male love because they have never experienced love from their father or another respected man, such as a male mentor. All such men know of love is associated with women. Sometimes young men become involved in sexual relationships in attempts to find love and to be loved. But this is not the love that meets their deepest need. They have not yet experienced being the "beloved," so they replace true love with a sexualized version. The beginning of a healthy male spirituality is to experience love from father and Father.

> *To be loved is the grounding of all human spirituality, but it is particularly poignant for men. It becomes the center point for all our experimentation and exploration.*

God's Love

In the New Testament, Jesus, in his native tongue of Aramaic, addresses God as "Abba, Father" (Mark 1:36). *Abba*, translated *father*, is in fact the most common address for God in the New Testament. It is used 170 times! *Abba* literally is an affectionate parental term like Papa or Daddy. It connotes compassionate tenderness, closeness, and nurturing. Ironically, all these are traditionally considered feminine characteristics.

The reason the Jews were so offended by Jesus' usage of the term was because it implied intimacy with the Almighty. They did not even pronounce the name of God, and here Jesus is addressing God with a familiar term of endearment. In Romans 8:14-16, Paul speaks of followers of Jesus as "children of God," and thus all are invited to call God "Abba."

Some people, especially some women, have difficulty calling God "Father" because of abusive or neglectful human fathers. Calling God "Abba" or "Father" is not about maleness; it is about relationship.[2] The importance of this name is that it is a personal, affectionate address. We could use "Mother" just as well when referring to God. God is not an "it." For men, it is important to experience divine father love, knowing that we are beloved and experiencing the tender and affectionate personal affirmation of Abba.

The story of the baptism of Jesus is a good example and model of this (see Luke 3:21-22). His baptism is very significant for his identity and the inauguration of his ministry. As John baptizes Jesus, the Holy Spirit in the form of a dove lights on Jesus and a voice from the heavens says, "You are my beloved son. I am deeply pleased with you" (author's paraphrase). What an affirmation for thirty-year-old Jesus as he begins his public work, as he becomes who he was meant to be!

God the father does not say this to Jesus after he has performed a miracle or delivered a profound sermon. God says it before Jesus has done anything. Would that every human son hear these words from his father as he becomes a man. Father love is not earned; it is given and received. That indeed is the foundation for a healthy and whole male spirituality.

The Youth Ministry and Spirituality Project (YMSP) has articulated four movements in the journey of the beloved.[3]

Father love is not earned; it is given and received. That indeed is the foundation for a healthy and whole male spirituality.

First, it begins in the heart of God because God is love. God places within us the desire to be loved. Jesus' desire to be "in my Father's house" (Luke 2:41-52) illustrates this yearning. Second, we are named as beloved as in the baptismal text just mentioned: "You are my beloved son." This is foundational to Christian formation. Third, Jesus claims his identity as the beloved while the accuser tries to tempt him with alternative identities and missions (see 4:1-13). Men continue to be tempted by various false visions of manhood rooted in selfishness and power. And fourth, Jesus is sent on his mission as the beloved (see 4:14-21). Jesus' first acts in the Gospels are acts of compassion, deliverance, and healing. Those who know they are beloved can go forth to genuinely love others. The YMSP applied this movement to youth ministry, but I believe it is also very applicable to the development of male spirituality and relationships between fathers and sons.

Father Love

Relationships with our parents during childhood have a profound influence on how we relate to God in later years. Therefore the experience of being the beloved by our divine Father is inextricably bound up with our experience of being

Father love is not only expressed with the words "I love you." It is also expressed through words and actions of respect and affirmation. beloved by our human father. Father love is not only expressed with the words "I love you." It is also expressed through words and actions of respect and affirmation.

Many fathers of my own father's generation were not particularly expressive of loving affection. A friend of mine said, "I knew that my father loved me, but he rarely said so in as many words." This is probably a typical testimony. It is certainly my story. I do not remember my father being anything other than loving, even if he did not always know how to show it or articulate it clearly. I think my dad eventually learned to say "I love you" to his children from my mother, who was much more expressive and articulate. Many men of my generation have made commitments to be more tangibly affirming and expressive of love to our sons.

Many men have not heard from their father what Jesus heard from his: "You are my beloved son." But it does not necessarily follow that we cannot or will not deeply experience divine Father-love as the necessary beginning of male spirituality. Author Donald Miller, who grew up without a father, writes, "Though some of us grow up without biological fathers, none of us grows up without our actual Father. That is, if we have skin, if we have a heart that is beating and can touch and feel, then all this is because God has decided it would be so, because he wanted to include us in the story."[4]

All men, regardless of their relationship with their earthly father, can experience being the beloved of the

Father. This is initiated by God and therefore transcends any lack of a human father. It is something that men pray for and long for. We have the promise of not only response, but initiative (see 1 John 4:10). It is the very nature of God to love. God *is* love. Men can experience being the "beloved son" whom our Father is deeply pleased with.

It is often difficult for men to let themselves be the beloved. The "letting" takes active courage. We not only are the beloved, but we become the beloved as we learn to trust God's love.[5] This was the struggle of Mackenzie Phillips in *The Shack*,[6] whose daughter was abducted, molested, and murdered. Mackenzie is compelled to return to the scene of the tragedy, almost against his will and better judgment. But there he receives a number of profound visions of God's loving presence in the midst of doubt and anguish. These visions are as real as life itself. Mackenzie's primary struggle is to experience God as a loving parent due to his own deprived childhood and his feelings of guilt about his daughter's abduction.

> *It is often difficult for men to let themselves be the beloved. The "letting" takes active courage.*

If Mackenzie had not taken this risk to return, he would never have experienced being the beloved of Abba. In the midst of tragedy, he learns to let God love him. Receiving and opening ourselves is an action, even if it is an action against our perceived masculine nature. It is actually the courageous beginning of manhood!

Visualizing things can help us experience what seems impossible to experience spontaneously. A profound verse of Scripture that led me into visualization was Zephaniah 3:17: "The Lord your God is with you, the warrior who saves you;

he will take great delight in you; in his love he will not scold you, but rejoices over you with loud singing" (paraphrased).

For those of us who are older and have left our dependent childhoods far behind, it can take some spiritual work to see ourselves as a beloved and dependent son.

I initially pictured God here as a mother singing her child to sleep, but as I have become a father to four children, I also picture God as a proud father singing over me, his beloved son, bear-hugging me in his strong arms, assuring me of his love, and belting out a tune of joyful pride.

For those of us who are older and have left our dependent childhoods far behind, it can take some spiritual work to see ourselves as a beloved and dependent son. But as the Scriptures say, "We must become like little children to experience the kingdom of God" (Mark 10:15, paraphrased). May we have the courage to find the little boy inside each of us who needs to be loved.

Being Fathers

This has implications for men as we reflect on our sonship, but also for men who are fathers or who will become fathers. I advocate the treatment Jacob gave to Joseph for all our sons, not only for a favored one. The fact that we do not practice polygamy and have a favorite wife as Jacob did gives us a head start on this.

Jacob's gift of a colorful coat is merely symbolic of the important spiritual reality of letting our sons know verbally, "You are my beloved son, and I'm pleased with you." We have a practice in our family that we never leave the house or let anyone leave the house without assuring those staying or leaving of our love. That is also how we send our sons into manhood.

Our oldest son graduated from high school last year. He was also baptized into Christ and the church around the same time. He's still not sure exactly what his calling is, so he spent the past year working, traveling, and volunteering. We've tried to assure him that he has already made the most important decision, to follow Christ in baptism and life, and that the rest of his decisions will come out of that primary calling. But it is hard for us as parents to let go of our children, even though it is a natural process. It is not hard to love my son, but it is sometimes difficult to show it in an unconditional way when his aspirations are different from what I had imagined for him. As a father, I say, "You are my beloved son, and I am deeply pleased with you, regardless of what you do."

Even those who do not have fathers can experience being the beloved through us. One of my friends teaches

Even those who do not have fathers can experience being the beloved through us.

at an alternative school for students who have trouble in the regular school system. He tells the story of his relationship with a student.

> After two years of teaching him, I realized that Hans was becoming addicted to heroine. In addition to all of the issues that come with that, he was also drawing some other students of the class into drug use. I told Hans that he either had to get help with his addiction, or he would be removed from the class. He was furious and accused me of not caring, but I assured him that I would be there for him. It was a case of tough love.

Hans reluctantly went into some drug counseling, and we drew some hard lines with him. Unfortunately a year later his addiction was again out of control. Hans was broke, lost his job, the relationship with his girlfriend was strained, and he wanted to kill himself. Hans visited me one night and we ended up going to Narcotics Anonymous together the next night and he made some positive connections there. Ultimately he moved away and I lost touch with him.

A few years later Hans showed up in my class unannounced, looking very much like a man. His stay was very brief. After a little bit of small talk he said he had come back to thank me. He was now married, owned a home, and had a full-time job. He quit all his drug use to be a positive influence for his son.

Hans experienced being the beloved of his teacher. It helped him grow into a man.

Listen to Love

Hear the words of the Lord to you: "You are my beloved son. I am deeply pleased with you, regardless what you have done, are doing, or will do." These are the foundational words for men's spirituality. You may have heard other words from your father or others in your life: "You are a weakling." "You'll never amount to anything." "You're stupid." But these voices are false.

You were loved long before our parents, teachers, spouses, bosses, and friends ever had the opportunity to say anything about you. You are beloved before anything else. Henri Nouwen urges us to "listen to that voice with great inner attentiveness. . . . Every time you listen with great attentiveness to the voice that calls you the Beloved, you will discover within yourself a desire to hear that voice longer and more deeply."[7]

Hear the words of the Lord to you: "You are my beloved son. I am deeply pleased with you, regardless what you have done, are doing, or will do." These are the foundational words for men's spirituality.

And as Desmond Tutu has said, "You don't know anything if you don't know you are beloved."

5

DREAMER

Joseph was a dreamer. Once he had a dream and he told his brothers about it. He said, "Listen to this dream I had. We were all out in the field, gathering bundles of grain. All of a sudden my bundle of grain stood straight up and all your bundles circled around it and bowed down to mine."

His brothers were upset and retorted, "So, you arrogant little twit. You're going to rule over us, are you? You'll be the big boss and we'll be your serving scum?" And they hated him all the more because of his silly dreams and the way he talked.

Some time later, Joseph had another dream, and again he told it to his brothers: "I dreamed another dream, and this time the sun and moon and eleven stars bowed down to me!"

Jacob overheard Joseph describing the dream and scolded him: "What's with all this dreaming? Am I and your mother and all your brothers all supposed to bow down to you? This doesn't make any sense." And now Joseph's brothers were really jealous. His father brooded over all this and wondered what it might mean. (Genesis 37:5-11; author's retelling)

To some it might seem that Joseph's special beloved status got to his head. His seemingly arrogant telling of his

69

dreams annoys me, but obviously not as much as it did his brothers and his father! Again, we have to get past these feelings to realize that Joseph's dreams give us a strong metaphor for male spirituality. The significance of dreams might not be a popular coffee-shop or even Bible study group topic, but the dreamer metaphor is worthy of some exploration.

Joseph's dreams show the importance of dreams for young men especially: dreams of themselves as chosen individuals, dreams of their potential, and dreams of who they can become.

Joseph did not manufacture his dreams; they were a gift of God, and we see Joseph living into his dreams later in life.

Joseph did not manufacture his dreams; they were a gift of God, and we see Joseph living into his dreams later in life. His dreams come true!

His dreams come true! They may seem arrogant in the telling, but they are part of what shapes the man Joseph. They prepare him and his family for what will be. Dreams are an integral part of Joseph's spirituality throughout his life. And dreams are important in spiritual renewal for all men. How can the metaphor of the dreamer enliven male spirituality today?

Dreamers in the Bible

In our materialistic and scientific society, dreams as a source of spiritual understanding and growth can seem intriguing but hopelessly archaic. For many, dreams are commonly interpreted as simply a mechanical, subconscious rehash of the previous day's experiences.[1] For others, they bring profound spiritual insight. What was your reaction when I announced that a dream convinced me of the appropriateness of the life of Joseph as a metaphor for male spirituality? You might have thought, "This guy is a professor at a Bible college and he's listening to his dreams? How quaint. Now let's get serious." I am serious. I am a scholar and an educator. And I stand in a fairly long and strong tradition of taking dreams seriously.

I still remember some dreams from my childhood and adolescence. Some frightened me, but others gave me hope and courage for the future. Dreams were also an important part of my adult healing process from childhood abuse. (I will address this in a later chapter.) Joseph was a dreamer and I am a dreamer, but we are not part of a small, loony minority. We are part of a biblical tradition that men need to reexamine today.

Joseph was a dreamer and I am a dreamer, but we are not part of a small, loony minority. We are part of a biblical tradition that men need to reexamine today.

In the Bible and in the early church, dreams were an important part of a person's relationship with God. Joseph is perhaps the best-known dreamer in the Old Testament, but he is joined by many others. See, for example, the stories of Jacob (see 28:10-22), Gideon (see Judges 7:13-15), and Solomon (see 1 Kings 3:4-6). It was a primary way God spoke to God's people: "When a prophet of the Lord is among you, I reveal myself to him in visions, I speak to him in dreams" (Numbers 12:6 NIV). The New Testament opens with another Joseph, the father of Jesus, being guided by dreams (see Matthew 1:20-25; 2:13-23).

Abraham Lincoln is reported to have said, "If we believe in the Bible, we must accept the fact that, in the old days,

God and his angels came to humans in their sleep and made themselves known in dreams."[2] We are no longer living in the "old days," but God still speaks in dreams.

Defining Dreams

Dreams were obviously looked at differently in ancient cultures, so it is difficult to know exactly what kind of dreams Joseph or others in the Bible had. Even in the Bible there is more than one way to look at dreams. We need to attempt to define dreams to get over our reluctance to embrace dreamwork as part of contemporary male spirituality. Although there may be other nuances and levels of meaning, for our purposes I want to differentiate between two types of dreams.

To get in touch with our dreams is to get in touch with God and our deepest desires that come from God.

First are the dreams we have while we are sleeping or in another subconscious state. Most commonly, we think of this kind of dream as "a succession of images present in the mind during sleep."[3] Sigmund Freud first alerted us to the significance of dreams as representing, in a symbolic way, the unconscious conflicts or desires of the dreamer.[4] Normally we dream about every ninety minutes as part of a normal cycle of sleep, although we do not necessarily remember or process all of those dreams consciously.

The dream world is constructed from images of things the dreamer has recently felt or experienced or from combinations of past memories. Yet it is an "altered state of consciousness," where the external world is almost completely eliminated and replaced by a deep inner world.[5] God speaks in this inner world. To get in touch with our dreams is to get in touch with God and our deepest desires that come from God.

Second, dreams can also be defined as strong spiritual intuitions that may be part of contemplative prayer or may come spontaneously in a waking or sleeping state. To differentiate, we could call these visions. These need to be distinguished from what we know as fantasizing. They also need to be distinguished from hallucinations in mental illness, where the person has lost the ability to distinguish between the outer world and the inner world.

Visionary dreaming fires the imagination and brings to bear the power of the Spirit on the outer world. The problems of the world are deep and wide, so if we have no dreams, we sink into despair. Walter Wink asserts that through intercessory prayer, the future can be opened up by people who fix their imaginations on a new "vision" and call it into being.[6] Or, as the biblical prophet cries, "Where there is no vision, the people perish" (Proverbs 29:18 KJV). With a vision, people will prosper. A vision for what could be brings the hope of the future to bear on the present.

Both kinds of dreams—the involuntary subconscious dreams and the intuitive visions of hope—can be part of men's spirituality. Both are gifts of God, whether they appear in the subconscious or come through developmental intuition. We do not make ourselves dream, but we can open ourselves to the reality and possibility our dreams con-

We do not make ourselves dream, but we can open ourselves to the reality and possibility our dreams contain. By becoming aware and conscious of our dreams, we begin to be open to God's transformation.

tain. By becoming aware and conscious of our dreams, we begin to be open to God's transformation.

What do men dream? What is the content of our dreams and visions? What do we dream for ourselves, our families, our communities, our world? A look at the dreams of Joseph, the biblical prophets, and spiritual men in history gives us some clues.

The Dream of the Young Man

Joseph's dreams during his youth are about him and his place in the world. One way we can understand the content of men's dreams is by looking at developmental theories. Developmental psychologist Erik Erikson has alerted us to the development of individual identity. During adolescence we come to see ourselves as separate from our parents and other authority figures. We begin to answer the question "Who am I?" The dream of the boy is to become a man.

James Fowler, a faith development expert and Methodist minister, has extrapolated on Erikson's theory and applied it to faith development. A most significant transition of faith formation is from what he calls the "synthetic conventional" stage to the "individuative reflective" stage of faith.[7] In the former stage, we practice faith as we have been taught by parents, teachers, or peers. Yet we move toward a faith that is processed internally. "Who am I?" is then defined not so much by those around us but by our personal reflection.

We undergo an internal process of questioning, reflecting, and "dreaming" about who we are. As boys, we see ourselves the way others see us, but as we grow toward manhood, we see ourselves more independently. We envision ourselves, who we are, and our place in the world. All of us dream of "being someone" as we answer the question "What do you want to be when you grow up?" A song lyric I wrote at age fifteen illustrates this dream.

> *As boys, we see ourselves the way others see us, but as we grow toward manhood, we see ourselves more independently. We envision ourselves, who we are, and our place in the world.*

I Want to Be Somebody

I wanted to be a policeman or a fireman
I wanted to be a big football star
I wanted to drive the fastest racing car
Most of all I wanted to grow up to be a man
In life I want to climb far
I want to be somebody

I wanted to be a movie star or a singer
I wanted to be a big money guy
I wanted to ride a big jet in the sky
Most of all I wanted freedom and power
In life I want to climb high
I want to be somebody

Now all I want to be is a Christian and a follower
I want to help people who are in need
I want to put Jesus number one indeed

Most of all I want to glorify my Saviour
Now anything is within reach
I want to be somebody

During the same phase of my life, I wrote in my journal, "I am a dreamer and could tell many dreams. I have a dream far off somewhere to be something, but that is only a dream." I would reply now, "Don't say it is only a dream. Live the dream!" The dream of a young man is to matter in the world and to have a place of significance.

The Dream Beyond the Self

But men's dreams are not only about the self. Little did the young man Joseph know the far-reaching implications of his dreams. These dreams were not only about his individual identity and place in the world. They were not simply dreams revealing the future events that would involve him and his brothers. These dreams were about how he would bring wholeness and healing to his family and to a country he did not even know about at the time.

Fowler's stages do not end with individuation but continue into the "conjunctive" stage and the "universalizing" stage. As we grow in faith, we integrate various relationships and life experiences—the painful, pleasurable and paradoxical—into our faith. Conjunctive faith is about putting together these sometimes disparate elements of our life experience. The end point of spiritual growth is when the self is completely unified with

God, others, and creation. Our ultimate dream is the "commonwealth of love and justice."[8]

Spiritual men do not merely dream of conquering the enemy in battle or of rescuing the beautiful princess. They dream God's dream of shalom for all and how they might participate in this dream. The vision might be about peace in the world or it might simply be about the well-being of the children in our care.

Martin Luther King Jr.'s famous "I Have a Dream" speech is a wonderful example of a man's dream that went beyond himself to his people and to his nation. It was probably fed by both types of dreams I have described— dreams that happen while sleeping or in another subconscious state and dreams that come from strong spiritual intuitions.

> I have a dream that one day on the red hills of Georgia, sons of former slaves and sons of former slave owners will be able to sit down together at the table of brotherhood. . . .
>
> I have a dream that my four little children will one day live in a nation where they will not be judged by the color of their skin but by the content of their character. I have a dream today!
>
> I have a dream that one day . . . little black boys and black girls will be able to join hands with little white boys and white girls as sisters and brothers. I have a dream today![9]

In Peter's Pentecost sermon, he quotes the prophet Joel: "Your young men shall see visions, and your old men shall dream dreams" (Acts 2:17 NRSV). This sermon inaugurated the new age of the Spirit in which all the old barriers of gender, age, and class would be erased. As men of the Spirit, may our dreams continue the communal dream of Martin Luther King Jr. and the vision of the prophet Isaiah.

> In the last days the mountain of the Lord's temple will be established as the highest of the mountains; it will be raised above the hills, and all nations will stream to it. . . . [God] will judge between the nations and will settle disputes for many peoples. They will beat their swords into plowshares and their spears into pruning hooks. Nation will not take up sword against nation, nor will they train for war anymore. . . .
>
> The wolf will live with the lamb, the leopard will lie down with the goat, the calf and the lion and the yearling together; and a little child will lead them. The cow will feed with the bear, their young will lie down together, and the lion will eat straw like an ox. The infant will play near the hole of the cobra, and the young child will put his hand into the viper's nest. They will neither harm nor destroy on all my holy mountain, for the earth will be filled with the knowledge of the Lord as the waters cover the sea. (Isaiah 2:2, 4; 11:6-9 NRSV)

Men need to be awakened to the spiritual significance of their dreams, whether they are dreams that occur during sleep or in other altered states, whether they are developmental intuitions and God-given longings, whether they are dreams about yourself and your place in the world, whether they are about the ultimate shalom of all things. Live your dreams!

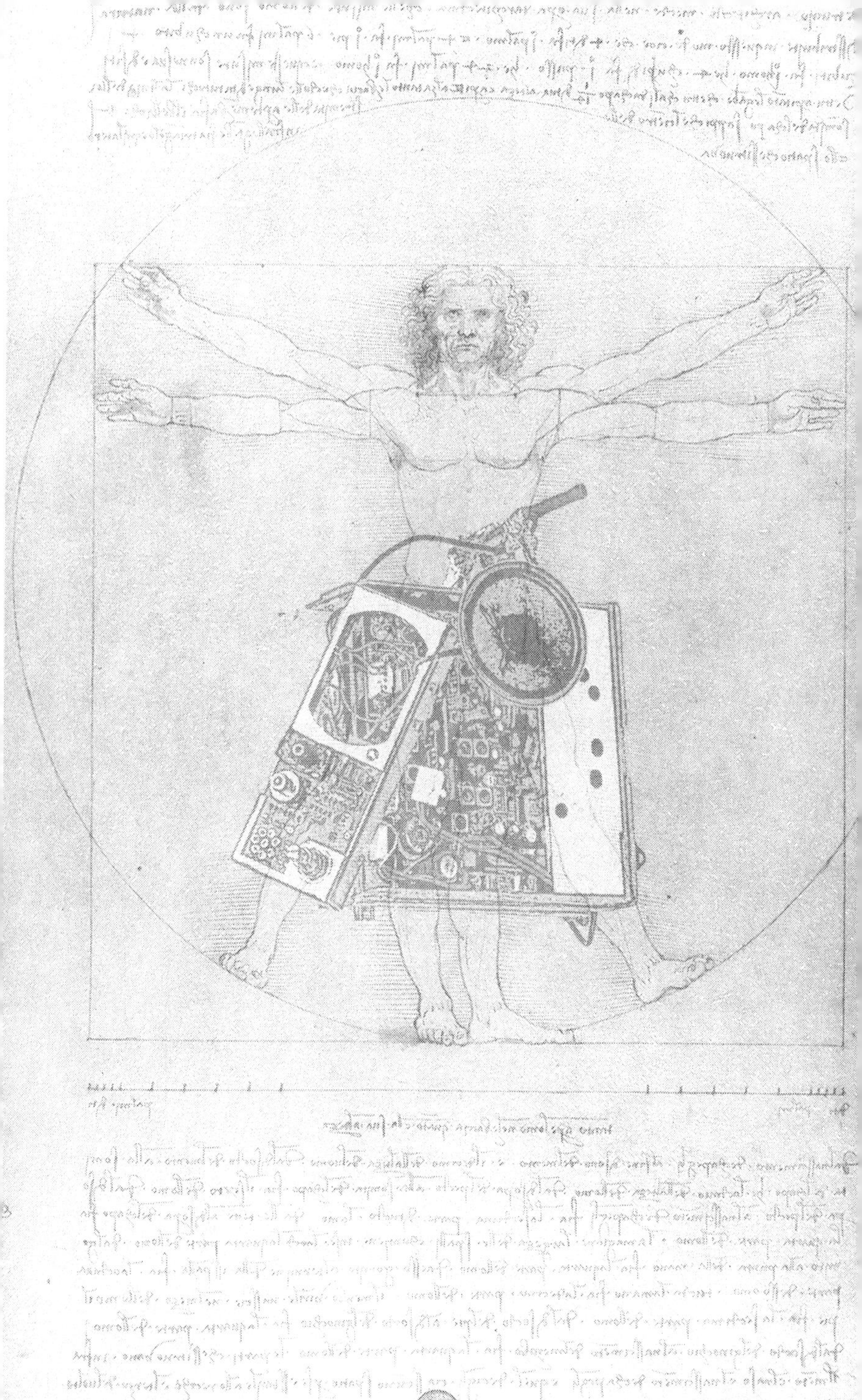

6

WOUNDED

One day Joseph's older brothers had gone off to
Shechem to look after the family's grazing livestock.
Jacob had not heard from them so he called Joseph,
and said, "Your older brothers are looking after the
herd in Shechem. I want you to go over there and see
how they are doing. Come back and let me know."

His brothers spotted him coming a long way off.
By the time Joseph got to them, they had devised a
plot to kill him. Here's how their conversation went:
"Here comes that dreamer boy with the fancy jacket!"

"Who does he think he is anyway?"

"Let's kill him and throw his body into one of
these old cisterns."

"We can tell everyone that a vicious animal ate
him up!" They laughed at that one.

"Yes, then we'll see what his big dreams come to!"

Reuben overheard his brothers talking like this
and intervened to save Joseph. "Murder is going too
far! He is our brother after all. You can throw him
into a cistern, but don't hurt him." He was thinking
that later on when they had left, he would come
back and rescue Joseph and bring him back home.

Joseph arrived all cheerful and unsuspecting.
"How's it going, guys?"

They didn't reply, but grabbed him, ripped off

his fancy coat, and threw him into the cistern. It didn't have any water in it, so Joseph landed in the dust in a heap of shock and bewilderment. "See if your dreams come true down there!" They laughed.

Joseph's heart sank. Indeed, there was no way for him to climb out. His dreams and his soul were literally in the pit of despair.

As the brothers were sitting down to eat their supper, they noticed a caravan of traders and camels on the horizon. The camels were loaded with spices, ointments, and perfumes to sell in Egypt. Judah said, "Brothers, I have an idea. We won't get any satisfaction out of killing Joseph and trying to conceal the evidence. Instead of killing him, let's get rid of him by selling him to these traders. He is our brother, after all."

His brothers agreed. "Good idea. That way he will be out of our faces forever, and we can honestly say we didn't lay a finger on him. And we can make a bit of money on the side!"

When the traders came by, the brothers flagged them down. They pulled trembling Joseph out of the cistern and sold him for twenty pieces of silver. The traders were happy to have Joseph with them as a slave on the way to Egypt.

Later Reuben came back from watching the flocks and checked the cistern. When he saw that Joseph wasn't there, he ripped his clothes and was beside himself with anger as he ran to the other brothers. "Where's the boy? You said you wouldn't kill him! What are we going to do now?"

They told him what they did and then decided what they would do to explain Joseph's disappearance. They took Joseph's fancy jacket and ripped it, butchered a goat, and smeared blood on the coat. They took the coat back to their father and said, "We found this behind some bushes. Do you recognize it? Do you think it is Joseph's jacket?"

Of course Jacob recognized it immediately. "It is my dear son's jacket," he wept in anguish. "A wild animal must have attacked him on his way to meet you. I can't believe it! My beloved Joseph torn to shreds!"

Jacob tore his clothes in grief, dressed himself in rags and mourned his son for days and weeks and months. Everyone in the family tried to comfort him, but he refused to be comforted. "I'll go to my grave mourning my son," he said, weeping uncontrollably. It was obvious he loved him deeply. (Genesis 37:12-34, author's retelling)

Joseph's lofty dreams come tumbling down to earth when he goes out to visit his brothers in the field. His brothers almost kill him, but instead throw him into a dry well and then sell him as a slave to some passing traders. It may be their own woundedness at not being beloved and special that leads them to this act of revenge. In the pit and in the slave train, Joseph is abandoned for dead by his brothers and by his father. Jacob never tries to find him but simply falls for the story and abandons hope.

Every Boy Hurts

Virtually every book on male spirituality I've read mentions some kind of wounding or abandonment, often by the father. Almost every author writes out of his experience of woundedness, and I am no different.

Although not every boy has a painful childhood, hurts stay with us and shape us in profound ways. It is not so much what exactly wounded us that makes the difference; how we respond to our wounds profoundly shapes our adult spiritual formation. We will deal with this again when we look at Joseph as a middle-aged man reflecting back on his past experience. For now, let's examine this seemingly universal experience of woundedness and what it means for men's spirituality.

It is not always a comfort to know that "everybody hurts," but it is good to remind ourselves as men that we are not immune to pain and that our pain is often instrumental in forming us spiritually.

It is not always a comfort to know that "everybody hurts," but it is good to remind ourselves as men that we are not immune to pain and that our pain is often instrumental in forming us spiritually. As a song by the group R.E.M. tells us, "Everybody hurts. You are not alone."[1]

It may have been that when a boy fell and scraped his knee, he heard, "Boys don't cry." And it may have been that he learned to shrug off pain and say, "It doesn't really hurt," and kept playing the game. But the reality is that the boy did get hurt.

Though physical pain is relatively easy to deal with, emotional and spiritual pain are much harder to bear. Both emotional and spiritual pain stay with us much longer and have the potential to do much more permanent damage. Men have learned to deny and repress pain, but it still rears its ugly head in ways that are hurtful to the self and to others. We may as well face up to it.

My Boyhood Wound

I was sexually abused as a young boy by my boyhood hero. My father was not able to play any sports, so this young man taught me all I ever knew about playing various sports. I give him credit for teaching me not only the skills of the games but also the courage of perseverance and the will to excel.

Men have learned to deny and repress pain, but it still rears its ugly head in ways that are hurtful to the self and to others. We may as well face up to it.

Unfortunately, this relationship was blemished on sleepovers at his house. There was no language of sexual abuse in my world at the time. There was no language for me to be able to tell someone or cry out to someone for help, or to say, "This is wrong. Don't do this to me." Therefore the pain went down deep inside for many years and got lost in the cobwebs of my memory until adulthood.

Kids who are abused sexually or otherwise lose their childhood innocence. They have been robbed of it and are left instead with a bag of scars and memories that they are unable to deal with. There are numerous self-protective "defense mechanisms" that victims like myself use to survive the trauma of abuse. An abused child is not able to feel the full emotions of pain, fear, or rage associated with abuse. If they could, they might go crazy. So what often happens is that the terrible memories and accompanying emotions are blocked or repressed involuntarily until adulthood.

Along with repression, there might be denial or rationalization of the experiences. "It happened so long ago." "Worse things have happened to others." "Maybe it was all just a bad dream." "He really didn't mean anything by it." "They were just jealous about my new coat." "There was nothing anyone could have done to stop it."

As an adult I was finally able to get in touch with the feelings of an abused child. The emotions that I was unable to experience as a child and as a teenager came roaring to life. It started with terrifying nightmares and irrational fears, and moved to feelings of deep pain, loss, and betrayal.

I was a powerful and successful man in the exterior world. I had a successful youth pastorate with a growing ministry and good relationships with my colleagues and the congregation. I had a loving and supportive wife, three healthy children, a house, and a minivan. What more could a man want? But pain does not discriminate. On the inside I became a little lost boy, feeling fully the terror and hurt of my childhood wounds for the first time. The following poem was written in the midst of those overwhelming emotions.

> little gary's dead
> he could not bear to stay
> he was murdered by his hero
> he'll never run and play
>
> little gary's dead
> we need to stop and pray
> the slaughter of an innocent
> haunts me every day

Sometimes we experience in the unconscious what the conscious disallows or cannot comprehend. Vivid dreams and nightmares are very common during intense times of healing as an adult. This poem describes a dream about one of my young sons, but it was really about me.

Powerlessness

Huge and yellow
block black letters
that say "Caterpillar"
it's a bulldozer
moving the earth
shaping exterior reality
impressively
making roads and ditches
with rumbling noise
and persistent movement
in all kinds of terrain

nearing a cliff
over the edge
it falls fast and hard
smashing, crashing
upside down
squished underneath
a boy driver
out of control
helpless
and needing
911

It is very difficult for men to admit to being a victim. Yet often victims become perpetrators if they do not deal with their wounds. It is sometimes easier for perpetrators of abuse to admit that they have hurt someone than to admit that they too were victims of abuse.

To be a victim seems to be the greatest threat to our "manhood." And yet our wounds can become the very place of our spiritual growth as we open ourselves to healing. But it takes courage. Henri Nouwen wrote, "Making one's own wounds a source of healing does not call for a sharing of superficial personal pains but for a constant willingness to see one's own pain and suffering as rising from the depth of the human condition which all [people] share."[2]

To be a victim seems to be the greatest threat to our "manhood." And yet our wounds can become the very place of our spiritual growth as we open ourselves to healing.

The Father Wound

Joseph experienced wounding by his brothers' cruelty. They themselves seem to have been unable to deal with their own woundedness from not being loved by their father the way Joseph was, and they lashed out at him as a result. This is now known as the "father wound." It is perhaps the most common and the deepest of male wounds.[3] I am thankful that I grew up with a father who never struck me or belittled me in any way. Not all men have been as fortunate.

The father wound may result from myriad situations: lack of a father through death or divorce, a father who is never around because of work or is aloof and distant when he is around, physical or verbal abuse, or simply lack of respect. The manly respect and honor that a boy gets from his father is what makes the boy a man.[4] Donald Miller writes poignantly about his own father wound in *To Own a Dragon*.[5] His primary dilemma was that he did not know what it meant to be a man because he never had a father to show him. We learn how to be a man from our fathers.

The father wound can be particularly deep. Some time ago a man whom I admired shared about his father wound through tears and sobs. All his life he could never measure up to the demands of his authoritarian father. He felt he could never work hard enough or be good enough to earn his father's approval. It was crushing his spirit, which was yearning to be a man. Decades later, in pastoral ministry, he was finally processing and coming to terms with the depth of his wound and how it had shaped his adult life.

Father wounds that are not dealt with might fester in unhealthy ways. Richard Rohr writes about a nun in prison ministry who couldn't supply enough cards for Mother's Day but had almost no requests for Father's Day.[6] With sadness, she realized that most of the men were in jail because they had never had a father who truly fathered them. They spent their lives trying to prove their manhood in devious and destructive ways.

In my previous work as a care worker and youth pastor, I often dealt with young men suffering from father wounds. They did not know how to relate to authority; they were often in trouble with the law; they suffered in other relationships and were often sexually deviant. "The father wound is so deep and so all-pervasive in so many parts of the world that its healing could well be the most radical social reform conceivable." Rohr writes.[7]

Recognizing Our Wounds

Thankfully not everyone experiences abuse or neglect from his father, mother, older brothers, or other trusted authority figures. But because adults are not perfect, most children are hurt or disappointed by them at some point. The process and depth of the healing corresponds with the nature and depth of the hurt or wound.

My focus has been on the wounds of the past. But men also deal with present wounds resulting from being rejected by their own sons, by the death or departure of a spouse, by condescension or humiliation from a superior at work, by debilitating illnesses—and the list goes on. Sometimes the wounds of men result from their own bad choices, failures, and sins. Repentance means turning from sin, whether it is ours or somebody else's that has affected us.

Sometimes the wounds of men result from their own bad choices, failures, and sins. Repentance means turning from sin, whether it is ours or somebody else's that has affected us.

Although some of our actions and pain may be rooted in the past, we can take responsibility and find healing for our present. It may be difficult, but we also know that God's grace is unlimited. It is sufficient even for us, especially in our greatest weakness (see 2 Corinthians 12:9). This is our calling as men: to recognize our weaknesses and our wounds so that in them we might find healing and strength from God. With a gracious God, wounds and weaknesses are not the end, but the beginning potential for growth and life.

As we will see later, Joseph was able to come to terms with his wound, and God turned it into a wonderful process of healing and reconciliation. For me, too, wounds became a source of healing and growth. We will return to this theme in a later chapter, but for now, it is important to accept and lovingly embrace the wounded boy that resides within us all. For some of us that may mean a process of forgiveness. For others it may be deep gratitude at being spared major hurts. For still others it might mean intense inner spiritual work with the help of a counselor or therapist. For all of us it means seeing our wounds as part of our

The Wounded Healer himself knows what it is to be wounded, and it is by his wounds we are healed.

spiritual formation. The Wounded Healer himself knows what it is to be wounded, and it is by his wounds we are healed (see 1 Peter 2:24).

7

JOURNEY

Joseph's brothers sold him for 20 shekels of silver to Midianite merchants. The young man left with these foreign traders, not knowing their destination. Joseph was scared; he had no idea where they were going or what they would do with him.

When the traders arrived in Egypt, they sold Joseph to Potiphar, one of Pharaoh's top officials.

God continued to be with Joseph even in Egypt, and things went very well for him as a result. He ended up living in the house of his Egyptian master, who recognized that God was with this young man in a special way and that everything he did turned out well. (Genesis 37:28, 36; 39:1-3; author's retelling)

Joseph is not only wounded and abandoned, but he is carried off to a far country. Later in his life Joseph sees the hand of God in this involuntary geographical move. It not only saved his life but the life of his entire extended family.

Leaving home is a necessary part of male growth, to "leave his father and mother" (Genesis 2:24) and establish a new home. A journey into the wilderness or a change of geography to an unknown locale, whether frightening or anticipated, has been an important source of spiritual healing and growth for many men.

A journey into the wilderness or a change of geography to an unknown locale, whether frightening or anticipated, has been an important source of spiritual healing and growth for many men.

Journey is a primary metaphor in male spirituality. Joseph did not exactly choose to go on his journey, but it did serve as an important shaping and saving event in his life. Sometimes our travels are chosen for us against our will, sometimes they just happen circumstantially, and other times we deliberately choose them. The common denominator is the journey.

It is interesting to compare again the two spiritual classics *Pilgrim's Progress* by John Bunyan and Teresa of Avila's *Interior Castle*. Although they were written a century apart and from different theological persuasions, it is noteworthy that the male writer used the epic upward journey motif while the female writer explored the various interior rooms of a mansion. Although both home and journey motifs are valuable for both men and women, the journey metaphor seems to be primary for male spirituality.

The journey, or the pilgrimage, has been integral to spirituality for centuries. For instance, the Israelites' exodus from Egypt and their journey through the wilderness have often been used as metaphors for the spiritual life. Yet journeys and pilgrimages can take various forms.

The Journey of the Young Man

The first journey is the young man leaving home. Erik Erikson was onto something when he articulated what he called the "identity moratorium."[1] His theory was that in the search for their identity, young men lay aside commitments in order to experience new things. This delay of commitment to a particular identity is what Erikson called the moratorium. It has many individual variations but often involves experimentation and travel.

Erikson's own moratorium was a hitchhiking trip across Europe; such trips have become symbolic of a young man's search for identity. The physical or geographical journey is not only a metaphor for growth in faith, a physical or geographical journey sometimes leads to growth in faith. As mentioned earlier, James Fowler built on Erikson's theory by focusing more specifically on faith.

Personal faith development sometimes also involves an individual journey away from familiarity. Faith becomes your own when it leaves home and branches out from its roots. Joseph needed to leave his favored position in order to grow. Young men also need to leave the faith of home to journey on their own. After the journey, their faith may look very similar to the faith of their parents, but the important movement has been the journey of personalization. The leaving, both geographically and spiritually, understandably often troubles the parent. But leaving is necessary for personal faith to develop.

Faith becomes your own when it leaves home and branches out from its roots. Joseph needed to leave his favored position in order to grow. Young men also need to leave the faith of home to journey on their own.

To stretch the travel analogy even further, growth in faith is like packing a bag for a trip. When I was a boy, my mother would pack my bag for me. But one summer I remember going to camp and insisting that I pack my own bag. I put in underwear, socks, shirts, and pants just like my mother did—maybe with a few different choices, but essentially the same. I also put in a bag of sunflower seeds, which were expressly forbidden in the camp registration form. The important thing for me was the process of packing my own bag. It is the same with faith. It is the process of "packing our own faith bag" that is important, regardless how different or similar it might look from that of our parents or elders.

With public transportation and the hostel system, world travel has become quite accessible for emerging adults. A friend of mine joined a singing group sponsored by a Christian organization that toured a few countries in Europe. He reflected on the impact of that experience and said, "I realize now that it entirely changed my life. It defined me as a different person; it gave me a tool with which I could cut off unpleasant memories and leave them in the past; it set me on a new course. And, in real way, defined my sense of 'home' for the future."

I never made it to Europe, but I did hitchhike a section of the Trans-Canada Highway. After graduation, my eldest son traveled across Canada for a few months with a friend and their musical instruments. Other than touching both coasts, they had no real plan or agenda except to experience different people, cultures, and locales before starting to pursue their vocations. This journey was important in the process of finding themselves as they interacted with different people and experienced new things. We noticed a significant change in our son's life when he returned. He had a new perspective, a new sense of independence, and self-awareness as a man.

I left home to attend Bible college and university, but my

first real travels happened after I was married at age twenty-four. After my wife finished her degree during the first year of our marriage, we decided to move from the familiarity of rural southern Manitoba to the urbanized world of central Ontario. We packed up all our belongings in a half-ton truck and traveled east. We had no jobs lined up, no apartment rented, no relatives or friends to be connected with. We just wanted an adventure. Or maybe I should say, I wanted an adventure and my wife went with me!

We camped for a few weeks until we found temporary jobs and an apartment. I ended up in graduate theological studies in Toronto and a part-time youth ministry position in Aylmer, Ontario. This time away from all familiar supports was instrumental in shaping who I was becoming as a man and who we were becoming as a couple.

Men of all cultures and economies experience some kind of leaving as part of their spiritual formation into manhood. Some cultures even have extensive rituals of male initiation. Often these involve sending the young men into the wilderness for a few days of authentic "survivor."

To our detriment, rituals of male initiation that were part of traditional cultures have largely been lost in secular western society. Rituals of initiation into manhood help provide a sense of separation from childhood, challenge men to grow, and allow them to be incorporated back into the community, now as men. Without these rituals, young men often create their own poor substitutes, such as initiation into gangs, which are often destructive of others and themselves.

To our detriment, rituals of male initiation that were part of traditional cultures have largely been lost in secular western society.

Effective rites of passage into manhood have numerous ingredients. It is important that young men see them as attractive and desirable and at the same time challenging. If rituals are too simple and easy, they are meaningless. Although the role of the father is central, other mature men can act as witnesses or sponsors in a ritual of transition into manhood. For me and my boys a camping trip of some kind has been a meaningful symbol of the movement toward manhood. I also give gifts of symbolic items such as a pendant, a watch, a Bible, or other unique item suitable to the personality of each of our boys, along with an appropriate explanation.

Besides a meaningful symbol or ceremony, there must also be opportunity for reflection and introspection connected to a rite of passage. It is a journey from boyhood to manhood, and it needs to be acknowledged and intentionally marked and celebrated by mature adults.

Circumstantial Journeys

For me, geographical moves have been an important part of my spirituality. As I look back on the three decades of my adult life, I see my spirituality closely tied to the places where I have lived. There have been remarkable connections between the geography of the land and the geography of my soul in each of the five provinces where I have lived as an adult, from Ontario to British Columbia.

There have been remarkable connections between the geography of the land and the geography of my soul in each of the five provinces where I have lived as an adult.

Some moves were carefully discerned, and others were

thrust on us. In retrospect, even the unexpected moves to unknown places turned out to be "what was best for me." The new place provided anonymity and safety for the healing of my soul.

With two provinces to the east behind us and, unknown at the time, two ahead of us to the west, I wrote the following poem as I trudged along the shores of the South Saskatchewan River in Saskatoon, wondering about the present place of transition. It is just as difficult to move spiritually as it is to move geographically, leaving the comfortable familiar and moving to the disconcerting unknown. And sometimes the two correspond, as they did in this case.

Good–bye/Hello

a closed door
memories
nurtured from the womb
his child I was
rebelled
yet always returned, the prodigal
poured, and then
all heart and soul, blood, sweat and tears
immersed
the ties were deep and strong
hating, loving, fighting, embracing
till the last drop
life sucked, lines drawn, doors closed
good-bye

an open door
wide, wide, wide, wide open

to stretching fields of virgin soil
and endless disconcerting opportunity
wind sweeps pulls up roots
back 500 years or more
overlooking the River
powerful, relentless to the sea
a world away
I take up my few possessions
to trudge along its banks
the journey home
somewhere
hello

Obviously, part of my geographical mobility may have been due to being in church ministry or my restless personality, but I think there might be some of this desire to be on the move in the male soul.

Sometimes the movement through unfamiliar internal terrain is brought on not by geographical moves but through pain, illness, or loss. Just as the circumstances of new geography vault us into spiritual journeys, so do the circumstances of suffering.

A friend of mine was hit by a sudden bout of bacterial meningitis, a disease that is disabling and potentially deadly. Long periods of hospitalization and respite at home became a journey of the soul—a journey into the unknown. Yet for my friend it was a journey toward wholeness and home despite not knowing how that might look. All of life looks different when a man has traveled through the valley of the shadow of death.

Recreational Journeys

In the male soul is a desire for adventure, exemplified by recreational journeys and wilderness wanderings of various kinds. Many men like to camp, hike, fish, or hunt in the wilderness. I heartily concur with the desire for adventure as a metaphor for male spirituality.[2]

I am not a serious mountain climber or backpacker, but when I am out on the trail, ascending a mountain in a lush west coast forest, it is not only my heart that is pumping and my lungs that are cleansed, it is also my soul.

When I am out on the trail, ascending a mountain in a lush west coast forest, it is not only my heart that is pumping and my lungs that are cleansed, it is also my soul.

Sometimes we become more in touch with God and our real selves when we go into the wilderness away from the routines of our daily lives.

A friend tells me of a trip to the Yukon where he and some companions were dropped off in the wilderness by a helicopter with their supplies, a few days walk from any human assistance. As he was confronted by the vast solitude of the wild, he was at the same time confronted by who he was. Positions, ranks, degrees, status, and salaries mean nothing when you are clinging to the edge of a cliff. It was an adventure into the self and into dependence on God and his companions. Our adventures and travels vary, but male spirituality is one that takes risks and is on the move. A recreational journey can be a wild ride both physically and spiritually.

Religious Pilgrimage

Religious pilgrimages have been a part of church practice

for centuries and are again becoming popular. Walking enables pilgrims to slow their spirit and to encounter unknown people and places intimately. Numerous books published recently have chronicled the pilgrimages of men.[3] Arthur Paul Boers says that "the pilgrimage nudged me to consider how I might live more focally. No surprise then that so many of us pilgrims on that route reevaluated our lifestyles."[4] A pilgrimage can help men put the rest of their life in perspective. It is a way of intentionally putting ourselves on a physical journey that assists or reflects the journey of the soul.

A pilgrimage can help men put the rest of their life in perspective. It is a way of intentionally putting ourselves on a physical journey that assists or reflects the journey of the soul.

I recently participated in a course entitled "Kentucky Holy Land Pilgrimage." Unfortunately, much of our travel was by air-conditioned coach, but we did have opportunity to walk a few miles to the Abbey of Gethsemani. We walked in silence and spent the day at the abbey in silence, listening only to the monks chant psalms at their appointed times.

For me, the pilgrimage took on an added poignancy because my luggage did not arrive until week's end. This is really what pilgrimage is about—leaving the structures and props we rely on for security, and venturing out. In my case, it was only a suitcase full of clothes. In everyday life, men rely on other material things, such as cars, jobs, buildings, computers, and power tools for our sense of having it all together. On a pilgrimage, we are stripped of these things and forced to depend on God more tangibly.

We know in our heads we are always dependent on God for sustenance, but a pilgrimage reminds us of this in a real way—particularly in my case, when all I had was the clothes on my back.

The Journey of the Soul

The important thing about the metaphor of the journey is not geographical movement, even if it seemed to be for Joseph and me and many others. A few years ago, when I was invited to speak at a men's prayer breakfast, I had an interesting conversation about journey with a man who had never left home geographically. He was in middle age, farming the same land as two generations of his family before him. He had married his childhood sweetheart, and they were raising a family in the same church and community as their ancestors before them. But he broke my stereotype of the "never been anywhere farmer." This man had traveled and was a pilgrim on a journey. He had experienced the world through personal tragedy, short-term service assignments, reading books, and conversations with people who were different from him. He was geographically rooted and content, but he was a traveler of the soul.

A few years later, with another unknown transition still to come, I experienced a profound sense of contentment one evening sitting in a campground in Golden, British Columbia.

In Golden

Up above and rising:
trucks
carrying timber and cars,

Wonder Bread—
gearing down for the Rockies east
with the Selkirk Mountains fading in the distant
west
a different world on either side.

I sit still:
warm tea cup
lantern glow
eyes longing
lonely
for where the road might lead,
but content
I've found my gold
right where I am . . .
in Golden.

The souls of men long for adventure. At the same time comes the paradoxical calling of contentment with where we are at present. So although the journey metaphor is primary for men, we also need to embrace the more feminine metaphor of home. Home is a treasure chest of spiritual warmth and safety whose depths must also be mined and explored. It is good for the male soul to travel, but it is just as good to stop to rest wherever our home may be. Joseph had dreams, but he never dreamt that his home would be in Egypt.

It is good for the male soul to travel, but it is just as good to stop to rest wherever our home may be.

I experienced an uncanny juxtaposition of home and journey in Swift Current, Saskatchewan, where we lived for only two years. As I commuted to Saskatoon for classes, whenever I crested the hill from the north and saw the lights of the city below, I had a feeling of "it's good to be home." At the same time, I felt it was a mere "stop for coffee" on the journey of life.

> My heart is home.
> Even though I journey
> I'll always be home
> with you.

Joseph was sold as a slave and eventually found safety in the foreign land of Egypt. His later descendants became a nomadic people who wandered the wilderness for forty years. I experienced numerous geographical moves for a variety of reasons, some planned and some unexpected. Others set out on symbolic journeys of pilgrimage. Some men travel to another continent in search of adventure, their identity, or a new life.

Wherever a man rambles, involuntarily or voluntarily, the promise of God's presence always goes with him.

In the Great Commission, Jesus seems to assume that his followers will be traveling to all nations. Wherever a man rambles, involuntarily or voluntarily, the promise of God's presence always goes with him: "Surely I am with you always, to the very end of the age" (Matthew 28:20 NIV).

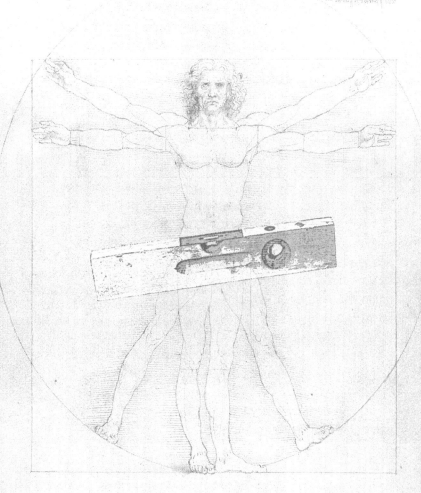

8

SEXUALITY

Potiphar became fond of Joseph and made him his personal assistant. He put Joseph in charge of all his personal affairs and turned over the management of his household to him. Because of Joseph, everything in Potiphar's home and business life prospered.

Joseph had grown to be a strikingly handsome young man. As time went on, his master's wife became infatuated with Joseph and one day attempted to seduce him. "Come to bed with me," she cooed.

"Absolutely not!" he said. "How could I, when your husband trusts me with everything he owns? He's put me in charge of everything and treats me like an equal. The only thing he hasn't turned over to me is you. You're his wife after all! How could I violate his trust and sin against God? I will not have sex with you!"

"Oh, but he is never at home and I am so lonely. . . . You are so good looking. . . . I want you so bad . . . please . . ." And with other words she pestered him day after day. But Joseph stood his ground, refusing to have any sexual contact with her.

One day it so happened that there were no other servants in the house. She grabbed Joseph by his cloak and begged him passionately, "Come have sex with me." Joseph left his cloak in her hands and ran out of the house. When she realized she had been foiled again and was holding his cloak in her hands, she screamed, "Rape! Rape! Servants! Come quick! This Hebrew tried to rape me, but I yelled and screamed, and he took off, leaving his coat behind."

She kept Joseph's coat for evidence and told her astonished husband the same story. "This Hebrew you hired tried to rape me!" When Potiphar heard this, he was furious and threw Joseph into jail.

Even in jail, God was still with Joseph. God was kind to him and put him on good terms with the head jailer. The head jailer put Joseph in charge of all the other prisoners so that Joseph was managing the entire prison. There was nothing to fear when Joseph was in charge. God saw to it that whatever Joseph touched turned out well. (Genesis 39:4-23; author's retelling)

The title of the chapter probably got every man's attention. What book on male spirituality could avoid a chapter on sexuality? The old saying says that "the way to a man's heart is through his stomach," but may be more accurately, "the way to a man's heart is through his genitals."

The sober truth is that sexuality and spirituality are deeply intertwined. It is uniquely so for men. "Sexual issues are always at the heart of masculine spirituality," according to Richard Rohr.[1] This is a sensitive and controversial subject that we need to address head on.

The story of Joseph and Potiphar's wife has always been a powerful one for me. Joseph is a sexual man, obviously an attractive young man, but one who is loyal to his male master and to God ahead of his ability to attract and

perform sexually. Joseph does not cease to be who he is—
a man with sexual desires and sexual attractiveness—but
he does not let libido dictate his behavior. Joseph stays true
to himself and is willing to accept the consequences without compromising his identity or his principles. Sexuality is
a powerful metaphor in this story, and it points us to some
important issues of male spirituality.

Sex and Sexuality

Sexuality is about more than having sex. I have a friend who
lives in Intercourse, Pennsylvania, in the heart of Amish
country. There is a thriving tourist industry built around the
apparent juxtaposition of conservative Amish people and
the sexually suggestive name of the town. You can imagine
some of the slogans on T-shirts, especially because the
neighboring town is Paradise.

But Intercourse was simply named for the intercourse,
or intersection, of two roads. Intercourse describes a
meeting. Sexuality is about the meeting of bodies but, more than that, it is about the meeting of whole people. A man is more than a penis and a human being is more than a

*Sexuality is about relation-
ship and deep connection
with another human being:
"bone of my bones and
flesh of my flesh."*

body. My body and my penis are very much a part of me
and my spirituality, but they do not define all that I am.

Sexuality is part of the creation story in the book of
Genesis. It was not good for man to be alone (see 2:18);
woman was created to be in relationship with man (see
v. 22). Sexuality is about relationship and deep connection with another human being: "bone of my bones and
flesh of my flesh" (v. 23).

The man and woman became "one flesh" in sexual union, but sex is more than two bodies made one: they "knew" each other (4:1 KJV). Later translations and paraphrases have replaced this "knowing" with "Adam lay with is wife Eve" (NIV), "Adam had sexual intercourse with Eve" (Living Bible), "Adam slept with his wife Eve" (The Message), "Adam made love to his wife Eve" (TNIV). This "knowing" is not at all euphemistic because it implies an intimate knowledge of one another, a complete nakedness, not only physically, but in every way. Sexuality as a metaphor for male spirituality is about making ourselves vulnerable to another, being in intimate relationship.

Our culture often defines sexuality as merely the chemistry that attracts people to each other and those acts that give physical pleasure. But this is a limited definition.

It's been said that women need emotional attachment for sexual fulfillment, but all men need is friction. Our culture often defines sexuality as merely the chemistry that attracts people to each other and those acts that give physical pleasure. But this is a limited definition. In his book *Sex God*, Rob Bell says that it is time to rethink our definition of sexuality:

> Our sexuality is all of the ways we strive to reconnect with our world, with each other, and with God. . . . Our sexuality, then, has two dimensions. First, our sexuality is our awareness of how profoundly we're severed and cut off and disconnected. Second, our sexuality is all the ways we go about trying to reconnect.[2]

According to this definition, genital intercourse is obviously one of the ways we connect as human beings, but it is not the whole story of our sexuality.

This definition explains why sexual acts without deep human connection are not only void of meaning but potentially destructive. Masturbation without any connection is ultimately unfulfilling. Pornography, which makes a pseudo-connection, is dehumanizing to those depicted, degrading of women as well as to the male consumer, and destructive to real relationships. Pornography is powerful and addictive. It is a god that spiritually enslaves men and abuses women. Sexual promiscuity and sexual affairs cheapen connections and end up destroying them. By its very definition, the sex act is intended to express a lifelong monogamous commitment. Without sexuality, sex is a lie.

Sexual Fidelity

I would like to add another word to our metaphor to create the perfect couple: fidelity. Fidelity is about faithfulness, loyalty, and allegiance. Put sexuality and fidelity together, and we have faithfulness in our relationships. The story of Joseph illustrates the sexual fidelity of a young man in his relationships with a sexually enticing woman, his own boss, and a God who actively cares for him.

Fidelity is about faithfulness, loyalty, and allegiance. Put sexuality and fidelity together, and we have faithfulness in our relationships.

Contemporary men find their sexual fidelity threatened on various fronts. Or, more positively, there are various ways that men can live out their spirituality through sexual fidelity. I see two options for followers of Jesus: celibacy or marriage. I assume, against the assumptions of our culture and with centuries of church tradition, that single people are celibate. I am a married man. I also have close friends who are married; who are single; and who have experienced separation, divorce, and remarriage. Each of them is unique in his sexual fidelity and spirituality. Let's explore these two primary paths of spirituality, keeping our definition of sexuality in mind.

Celibacy

In a discussion with the Mission Springs Group (see preface) about who we thought were spiritual men, many of those named were celibate single men such as Thomas Merton and Henri Nouwen. Saints such as Francis of Assisi and Ignatius of Loyola were also celibate, at least after taking their vows. Celibacy, although restricted to the called few, was assumed to be the more spiritual choice until the Protestant Reformation.

Because of the abuse and corruption of celibacy in the Middle Ages, reformers such as Martin Luther worked hard to suggest that celibate monasticism was not an appropriate way of life for Christians. This negative attitude toward celibacy has continued, especially in our sex-saturated culture.

None of the contemporary evangelical men's books I've surveyed even mention singleness as an option for men. The assumption seems to be that men need to be having sex to be whole and fulfilled.

Many evangelical Protestants do not have a healthy and dignified view of singleness and celibacy today, especially not for men. None of the contemporary evangelical men's books I've surveyed even mention singleness as an option for men. The assumption seems to be that men need to be having sex to be whole and fulfilled. Another assumption is that celibate single adult males are too passive and nice, and that's why they never get their princess.[3]

It seems that the only time a mention of celibacy comes up is when certain churches require it of homosexuals. Yet they don't even suggest it as an option for mature heterosexual men. We need to have a discussion about the pleasure and dignity of celibacy, regardless of sexual orientation.[4] Authors Ted Grimsrud and Mark Thiessen Nation disagree on their view of homosexuality, but they agree that sexual intercourse is reserved for marriage.[5] I would add that fidelity in sexual relationships is indeed the primary issue for men's spirituality.

Our conversation about celibacy starts by reading the Bible. Paul definitely speaks of sexuality and spirituality. Interpreters sometimes say Paul has a negative view of marriage, but I believe he has a positive view of sexuality for celibate singles and for married couples.

First Corinthians 7 is a key text used when discussing sexual fidelity. Paul's negative reason for getting married is so that a man doesn't destroy himself with lustful passion (see v. 9). His reason for singleness is more positive: single men are able to devote themselves solely to the work of the Lord (see v. 32). The overwhelming theme of this text is fidelity in the state to which God has called you. For the Corinthians, "it was faithfulness to their vows that mattered in the end, not the particular state of life."[6] The way of celibacy is a way of becoming more Christlike, because those who are celibate are free to love all people rather than being consumed with those closest to them, such as spouse and children (see vv. 32-35).

Celibacy is often a vow made for life, but it can also be a vow for a particular period of time or "until marriage." Joseph was a young man who eventually got married. Yet he showed remarkable sexual fidelity to himself and others in the situation with Potiphar's wife. Young men today face similar sexual temptations, although the temptations take myriad forms through the media. The response to such temptations is not a dispassionate "just say no" but a commitment to value and protect the deep connection that happens between people who are involved sexually.

Sex is not mere biology. It is a deeply spiritual and emotional as well as a physical union.[7] We make ourselves vulnerable and completely open to another person in sex. Waiting for sex until marriage is not old-fashioned prudishness. It is recognizing the deep intersection of spirituality and sexuality, and it is giving sacred dignity to our future sexual partner. Donald Miller advises young single men that "in a family, in marriage, it's important that sex be something special, and as men, it's important we take initiative in protecting it. Those habits start now."[8]

Waiting for sex until marriage is not old-fashioned prudishness. It is recognizing the deep intersection of spirituality and sexuality, and it is giving sacred dignity to our future sexual partner.

Both celibacy and marriage are honored callings, but celibacy is hardly considered by most young men setting out on the path of life. The recent "new monasticism" movement is an example of both celibacy and marriage being embraced in faith communities. Perhaps the most well-known single man in this movement is Shane Claiborne of Simple Way in Philadelphia.[9]

It would be good if celibacy was not only seriously considered by young men, but if it were lifted up as a high and worthy calling. May the church give support and honor to those who have chosen it.

Marriage

The majority of men in our society are married, have been married, or hope to be married. Is it possible to be a happily married man and a deeply spiritual man? In 1 Corinthians 7, Paul says it is difficult, but I'm quite sure it is possible. Rather than marriage and family being in opposition to spirituality, they can be integrated. Ephesians 5:21-33 is a good balance to 1 Corinthians 7 in the development of a Pauline view of marriage. Here Paul says marriage between a woman and a man is mysteriously like the relationship between Christ and the church.

Human sexuality is part of being created in the image of God that sets us apart from animals. Sexual intimacy in marriage is a precious and pleasurable gift from God,

A good and lasting marriage and continued sexual enjoyment is a gift from God.

but it is also delicate, and it takes careful diligence and self-sacrifice. I have found this to be true in our marriage. We've had our mountaintops and valleys. A good and lasting marriage and continued sexual enjoyment is a gift from God.

> This moment
> like a perfectly cut diamond
> I hold precious
> in my hands
> trembling

> because it is not mine
> but a freely given gift
> fragile and temporal.

Marriage is about sex, companionship, and the possibility of children. But even more than that, "marriage tells us something about God."[10] It is a sacred, exclusive, loyal, lifelong, mutually submissive, mutually respecting, love-based commitment. In that sense marriage reenacts God's fidelity to us. As God is faithful to us, we are faithful to each other. When a couple gets married, they speak vows of fidelity to each other, "forsaking all others . . . in sickness and in health . . . till death us do part." When fidelity in human relationships mirrors fidelity in our relationship with God (see 1 John 4:7-12), sexuality and spirituality embrace.

When fidelity in human relationships mirrors fidelity in our relationship with God sexuality and spirituality embrace.

How do men express fidelity in marriage? Our pre-marriage counselor said marriage is like gluing two pieces of paper together. We are pasted! If you try to rip the pieces apart, they tear beyond recognition. Obviously, sexual fidelity in marriage is primarily expressed by staying with and enjoying your wife.

Next year it will be twenty-five years for my wife and me. Our sexual relations have changed and deepened over the years, and we are more in love than ever. I could share a few poems from a collection I have written for my wife, but part of fidelity is the privacy of certain things. A few words of Scripture will suffice.

Drink water from your own cistern,
running water from your own well.
Should your springs overflow in the streets,
your streams of water in the public squares?
Let them be yours alone,
never to be shared with strangers.
May your fountain be blessed,
and may you rejoice in the wife of your youth.
A loving doe, a graceful deer—
may her breasts satisfy you always,
may you ever be captivated by her love.
(Proverbs 5:15-19 NIV)

Fidelity will not always be sex and fun. Sometimes it might be simple faithfulness in daily ordinary routines, mutual allegiance against outside threats, or mutual perseverance through difficult situations. One example of male fidelity in marriage is a man I knew whose wife was paralyzed from the neck down. Too many men in midlife have abandoned their wives for younger women who can "give them the sex they need." But this man cared for his wife day in and day out, and I'm sure experienced increasing depth in their relationship in spite of her disability. That is sexual fidelity.

Marriage has fallen on hard times of late in North America, with abuse, violence, separation, divorce, adultery, and extramarital affairs all on the increase. We do not live in paradise.

Although Jesus affirms lifelong fidelity in marriage, he acknowledges that there is a place for divorce in limited circumstances (see Matthew 5:31-32). Jesus' allowance of divorce in cases of infidelity only highlights the sacredness and importance of marital faithfulness. Sexual infidelity is a complex and difficult issue, and those who have experienced it require much pastoral care and deep, long processing.

Men and women are sometimes unfaithful. Yet God is faithful to us during our own unfaithfulness. The possibility of remarriage to begin a new relationship of fidelity speaks of God's faithfulness in redemption.

Fidelity for All

This chapter is not primarily about sexual morality or sexual behavior but about sexual fidelity as a metaphor for male spirituality, a fidelity illustrated by one brief but dramatic moment in Joseph's life. As I said earlier, fidelity is about faithfulness, loyalty, and allegiance. Joseph's sexual fidelity is grounded in his spiritual integrity and commitment to God.

This metaphor of sexual fidelity challenges all men—regardless of sexual orientation or marital status—toward a bodily, rooted, and connected spirituality lived out at the table, on the sidewalk, and in the bedroom.

> Jesus does not offer a case for either marriage or celibacy. If there is a theme that goes through the gospel accounts, it is that Jesus has a view toward a much larger goal: faithful discipleship to Christ himself. Such faithful discipleship takes place in the context of faithful marriages or faithful service as celibates in the kingdom of God.[11]

Both celibacy and marriage "require lifelong vows to one person or several people, because living out those vows teaches a person how to love. To paraphrase Dorothy Day, vows remind us that as Christians we are not called so much to be successful in our loving as to be faithful to God, whom we know as love."[12]

Single people and married people need each other to help them live out their vows, their callings. Men in each stage and state of life have gifts to offer each other. The gifts of single men especially have been underappreciated in Protestant churches. My call now is for communities of faith to be more intention-

Single people and married people need each other to help them live out their vows, their callings. Men in each stage and state of life have gifts to offer each other.

al in supporting a man toward a robust sexual fidelity in whatever state of life he finds himself.

Our sexuality and spirituality are inextricably intertwined. Men (and women) are whole people; we cannot extract our spirits from our bodies or our bodies from our spirits. It is a holistic, sensual, bodily, social, sexual spirituality. Sexual fidelity is about loyalty and depth in all our relationships with our marriage partners, relatives, friends, and colleagues.

9

GIFTS

Some time later, the cupbearer and the baker of the king of Egypt did something that offended their master. Pharaoh was furious with them and threw them into jail. It just so happened that it was the same jail that Joseph was in. And Joseph was assigned to get them settled in custody.

After they had been in jail for a while, both the cupbearer and the baker had a dream the same night. When Joseph was doing his rounds the next morning, he noticed that they were looking very disoriented and depressed. "You guys look awful. What's wrong?" he asked them.

They said, "We both had dreams last night and have no clue what they mean. There's no one around who can help us out. We're troubled."

"Don't give up so soon!" Joseph said. "Dreams and interpretations come from God. Tell me your dreams."

The cupbearer went first. "In my dream there was a grapevine with three branches loaded with ripened grapes. I picked the grapes and squeezed them into Pharaoh's cup and gave the cup to Pharaoh."

"This is the meaning of your dream," Joseph replied. "In three days you will get out of here and you will get your old job back. You'll be serving Pharaoh wine just like you used to do. But do me one favor: when things are going well for you again, tell Pharaoh about me so I can get out of here as well. I was kidnapped in the land of the Hebrews, and I've done nothing to deserve being put in jail."

When the baker heard how well the meaning of his buddy's dream turned out, he couldn't wait to tell Joseph his dream. "In my dream I saw three wicker baskets on my head with an assortment of breads and pastries I had baked. Birds were flying over and picking at them from the basket on my head."

Joseph cleared his throat. "The three baskets are three days." He paused. "And in three days Pharaoh will cut off your head, impale you on a post, and birds will come pick at your flesh."

On the third day it was Pharaoh's birthday, and he threw a big party for all his officials and servants. He remembered the two he had imprisoned and brought them out. Pharaoh gave the cupbearer his old job back, and beheaded and impaled the baker on a post. Joseph's interpretations turned out exactly as he had said. But the cupbearer, in his joy, completely forgot about Joseph languishing in prison.

Two years passed, and Pharaoh had a dream: He was standing by the Nile River when seven good-looking, healthy cows came up out of the river and started grazing on the marsh grass. Then seven ugly cows, all skin and bones, came up out of the Nile and ate up the seven healthy cows. Then Pharaoh woke up with a start and realized it was a dream.

He went back to sleep and dreamed a second time: Seven heads of grain, full-bodied and lush, grew out of a single stalk. Then seven more heads of grain sprouted up, but they were thin and dried out. Then the thin heads of grain gobbled up the full, healthy heads of grain. Pharaoh woke up again, troubled by his dream.

By morning, Pharaoh was in a cold sweat, upset by his dreams. He called for all the magicians and wise men of Egypt. He told them his dreams, but they were mystified and unable to interpret them.

The cupbearer overheard their conversations as he was serving, and he suddenly remembered Joseph. He said to Pharaoh, "I just now remembered something I should have told you a long time ago. Remember when you were mad at me and the baker and put us in prison? When we were there, both of us had dreams the same night and there was this Hebrew slave who worked for the captain of the guard. He had a special gift for interpreting dreams. We told him our dreams and he told us the meaning. Things turned out exactly the way he said." (Genesis 40:1-23; 41:1-13; author's retelling)

Each man has gifts. One of Joseph's gifts was dream interpretation. Joseph did not interpret his own dreams but those of his fellow prisoners, who were troubled by them. Later on he also interpreted the dreams of the Pharaoh of Egypt and subsequently becomes the ruler in Egypt, fulfilling his earlier dreams.

Joseph is concerned for his own well-being, but his gift is for the benefit of the community (except for the poor baker!), not for self-advancement. It seems he also has the gifts of administration, discernment, and compassion. God uses all of Joseph's gifts in ways beyond what his lot in life might have predicted. Gifts are from God for the benefit of others. Men's spirituality is about discovering, developing, practicing, and sharing our gifts.

Spiritual Gifts

My focus will not be so much on the specific gift of dream interpretation but on the spiritual gifts of men in general. We begin with the metaphor of gift and pass it around the circle. What are the spiritual gifts of men? Do men have unique gifts that women don't have? How do men practice spiritual gifts in ways that are uniquely masculine? What is the ultimate purpose of spiritual gifts? How can we share our gifts?

Some twenty-two spiritual gifts are listed in the New Testament. They primarily come from four different texts: Romans 12:3-8; 1 Corinthians 12:7-11, 27-31; Ephesians 4:7-16; and 1 Peter 4:7-11. The gifts include hospitality, service, speaking, apostleship, prophecy, evangelism, equipping, teaching, miracles, healing, helping others, administration, tongue speaking, interpretation of tongues, wisdom, knowledge, faith, discernment, encouragement, generosity, pastoral leadership, and mercy. I have seen and used gift discernment tests on which people check off various statements about this compilation of gifts. These can be helpful, but they also are restrictive. There are so many other spiritual gifts—for example, dream interpretation—that I won't begin to try to list all of them.

Some teachers and preachers have taken pains to create a separation between spiritual gifts and natural gifts, or talents. But all gifts are spiritual and all gifts are from God. All gifts can be used for good or ill, for self or others, whether it is singing or preaching, administrating or editing. It is also not necessary for us to speculate about how or when or where people get them. The Spirit gives the gifts to each one as the Spirit pleases (see 1 Corinthians 12:11).

Men, Women, and Gifts

What are the spiritual gifts of men? I think this is a rhetorical question, but it needs to be asked. Are there unique spiritual gifts that only men have? None of the texts above, or any other biblical texts, make any differentiation. All the gifts are for men. All the gifts are also for women. In the past, and unfortunately still today, some churches restrict certain gifts to men only, namely some of the leadership gifts, while others are for women and men. I know of no one who says there are some gifts that are for women only. Allowing women to use their gifts of leadership has profound implications for male spirituality. It is important for male spirituality and also for the sustainability and growth of the church.

At Pentecost there was a special visitation of the Holy Spirit with tangible signs (see Acts 2). As a spokesperson, Peter got up and explained that these strange and wonderful events are the fulfillment of Joel's ancient prophecy that the Spirit would be poured out on all people. Old barriers and walls that once stifled and restricted the Spirit are now broken down.

> In the last days, God says,
> I will pour out my Spirit on all people.
> Your sons and daughters will prophesy,
> your young men will see visions,
> your old men will dream dreams.
> Even on my servants, both men and women,
> I will pour out my Spirit in those days,
> and they will prophecy. (Acts 2:17-18, quoting
> Joel 2:28-29).

One of these walls is the barrier of gender. There is now no discrimination according to gender. It is very significant that the writer of Acts says both "sons and daughters will prophesy," especially considering the time and place this was happening. Prophecy is the gift of preaching, of proclaiming God's words. Prophecy is a sign that God is speaking to people. And now God would speak through all people, regardless of gender. The barrier of gender would no longer be relevant in the age of the Spirit. Male or female was no longer an issue for ministry. God would now speak through one and all. There are numerous examples of this happening in the book of Acts, such as Priscilla teaching the great preacher Apollos (see 18:24-26) and Phillip's daughters prophesying (see 21:8-9).

Pentecost has some implications for us today. First, in Christ there is no young or old, male or female, white collar or blue collar, or any other category for that matter; all are one in Christ (see Galatians 3:28). Second, all are gifted—rich and poor, young and old, men and women. No gifts are restricted for only certain people. The gifts of preaching and leadership are not only for educated, middle-aged men. The Holy Spirit gives and determines the gifts, not us. And finally, all people are ordained. Both women and men are called to ministry. In fact, all of God's people are ministers and priests (see 1 Peter 2:9). If men can be ordained, so should women.

Men Share the Gift of Leadership

What implications does this have for men's spirituality? Gifts are given for the common good (see 1 Corinthians 12:7). As Joseph modeled, the nature of spiritual gifts is that they are to be shared. Spiritual gifts are the gifts that keep on giving. "Whatever we have been given is supposed to be given away."[1] This sharing of gifts is not only about practicing gifts on behalf of others, but also about letting others practice the gifts they have been given.

Men have too often said, "The gift of leadership is only for us to practice." Men have been given the gift of leadership, but we have not shared it with women, thus the gift has been squandered. Author Sally Morgenthaler says it well:

> Leadership in a truly flattened world has no precedents. Never in the history of humankind have individuals and communities had the power to influence so much so quickly. The rules of engagement have changed, and they have changed in favor of those who leave the addictive world of hierarchy to function relationally, intuitively, systemically, and contextually. Male leaders—yes, even the male leaders of the entrepreneurial churchdom—know this at their core. They realize they're playing a deadly endgame [and] that the hierarchical clock is ticking. More than that, however, they have a deep knowledge of another way of being, though they may rail against it, retreating for comfort into cardboard cutout versions of both leaderships and masculinity. But if they're honest, they know they have tasted the new essence that is required of leadership now. They know it in the recess of their boyhood memories and in the experience of intimacy, art, music, story, film, hospital prayers, and all that human beings do best, together. Those who are up to the challenge of the new world will draw on

that deep knowledge. And they will look to the marginalized—including women—not necessarily as necessary evils in a politically correct world, but as their own leaders, mentors, and guides. The brightest will finally dump the myth of the great man, park their egos, and follow the Great [Human Being] into the relinquishment of power.[2]

Men have hoarded certain leadership gifts and they have stagnated in the pool of masculinity for too long. Women practice this gift differently than men do, and we need both men and women to discover, develop, and practice the gift of leadership. As men take a risk, let go, and empower women as leaders, we will in return be enlivened by the fresh flowing water of the Spirit. We will become free to be ourselves, men of the Spirit, not clinging to a special status for our identity, security, and strength.

The church I am a part of encourages all people to use their gifts, including women who have gifts of leadership and preaching. In fact, our senior pastor is a woman. My wife has leadership gifts and has served on the church council along with other men and women. I prefer to teach Sunday school and preach on occasion. Along with other men in our congregation, I feel free to be who I am called to be, without feeling pressure to take on leadership roles I am not gifted for. Sharing the gift of leadership with women impacts men's spirituality in a positive and constructive way by giving us the spiritual humility and strength to be equal partners in the work of the church.

Male Practice of Gifts

It is not the gifts that make men and women different; it is the practice of the gifts. The differences are due to both cultural and biological factors and their interaction, but there are differences between how women and men practice their gifts. The Myers-Briggs Type Indicator attests to this difference. Research shows that there is no gender difference on any of the four bi-polar scales of this personality tool,[3] except the one on how people process information to make decisions. Generally, men tend to make decisions using logic and thinking. Women tend to process through interaction and feeling.[4] This might also give us an indication of how men and women generally practice their spiritual gifts.

I am not aware of any research into male-female differences in the practice of spiritual gifts, but I have made some anecdotal observations from observing the work of the church. I have worked with a male pastor and a female pastor. The female pastor was more nurturing and collegial in her approach, and the male pastor was more task-oriented and decisive in his approach. I also know a couple who both have the gift of service. He goes to the location with his equipment and efficiently gets the job done. She calls up a number of people to meet together to plan and brainstorm before getting to the task. The process and the work become a lively social affair where there is lots of conversation and laughter. Not all men and women are like this, but I think this illustrates a basic difference in how gifts are practiced.

Men tend to be more task-oriented in the practice of their gifts. Unfortunately, tangible tasks have sometimes been labeled as unspiritual activities. Yet if we return to the list of spiritual gifts mentioned earlier, we see task-oriented gifts, such as service, discernment, and administration. Spiritual growth is often seen as primarily relational. Is there such a thing as a task-oriented spirituality? Yes! It is true that Christian faith is relational, but "getting a job done" could also be considered a spiritual activity if we embrace a holistic definition. Maybe more men would see themselves as spiritual people if "tasks" were seen as spiritual activities. And with that recognition might come spiritual growth.

A man and woman may share the same gift, but they practice it in different ways. One way is not better or worse than the other. In fact, men need women and women need men as they practice their gifts.

A man and woman may share the same gift, but they practice it in different ways. One way is not better or worse than the other. In fact, men need women and women need men as they practice their gifts. Being different is an essential part of being the body of Christ, as Paul goes on to explicate in 1 Corinthians 12. Church and family life is to be complimentarian *and* egalitarian in the true sense of both words.

10

BUILDER

Pharaoh sent for Joseph with some urgency. The guards quickly brought him from jail, cleaned him up, gave him a haircut, and brought him before Pharaoh.

"I had two dreams," Pharaoh told Joseph. "My cupbearer tells me that you can interpret dreams."

"No, it's not me," Joseph answered, "but God. God will tell me the meaning of your dreams."

So Pharaoh described his dreams to Joseph—emphasizing especially how gaunt the skinny cows looked, even after they had eaten the fat ones. When he had finished telling the second dream, Pharaoh was exasperated. "And none of Egypt's best sorcerers and sages could make any sense of these dreams!"

"Both dreams mean the same thing," Joseph said. "God is telling you what will happen in the future. This is what will happen: Seven years of plenty are on their way throughout Egypt with good crops, lots of food, and prosperity. But then there will be seven years of total famine. The crops will dry up and the food cupboards and the storehouses will be ravaged. The fact that you dreamed the same thing twice emphasizes how sure God is that this will happen—and it will happen soon."

There was a long pause as the words sank in, and Pharaoh wondered what he should do next.

133

As if on cue, Joseph said, "Look for a wise and experienced man, and put him in charge of managing the country's food supply. Also, you need to appoint regional managers throughout Egypt to organize things during the years of plenty. Their job will be to collect food during the good years and stockpile it in the towns so that it can be distributed when the famine hits Egypt. This way the country won't be devastated when the famine comes."

Pharaoh and his officials nodded at each other as if to say, "This guy really has his head screwed on straight; he knows what he's talking about."

Pharaoh verbalized it: "Isn't this the man of the hour? We won't find anyone who has God's spirit in him like this; he has obvious insight and administrative skills."

So Pharaoh addressed Joseph. "We want you. You're the man for us. God has given you insight into my dreams and also the wisdom to know what to do. From now on, you will be in charge of all my affairs; everyone else will report to you. I'll be the only one who will be over you in Egypt."

Pharaoh commissioned Joseph by removing the signet ring from his finger and slipping it on Joseph's hand. He outfitted him with the finest wardrobe and gold jewelry. Joseph had a chariot at his disposal, and when he rode around, people bowed down and shouted, "Make way!" What a step up from where he had been just a few days ago. Joseph was now in charge of the entire country of Egypt.

To symbolize the transformation, Pharaoh gave Joseph an Egyptian name, Zaphenath-Paneah, which means "God speaks and lives," because that had been Pharaoh's experience of Joseph. He also gave him an Egyptian wife, Asenath, the daughter of Potiphera, the priest in On. Joseph was all set up to begin his duties over the land of Egypt. And all this at only thirty years of age!

Joseph didn't waste time getting on the job. During the next seven years, the land produced bumper crops. Joseph organized the gathering and storing of all the surplus grain. There was so much grain that he finally quit keeping track of it. The storehouses overflowed.

During these good years, Joseph and Asenath had two sons. Joseph named the first Manasseh (forget), saying, "God made me forget all the hardships of my boyhood." He named his second son Ephraim (double blessing) because of all the prosperity Joseph now had, even though he had come to Egypt as a slave.

Then the good years of prosperity ended and the seven years of famine hit hard, just as Joseph had predicted. As the effects of the drought spread throughout Egypt, people began crying out to Pharaoh in distress. "Give us grain so we can make bread!"

Pharaoh said, "Go to Joseph and follow his orders."

As the famine got worse, Joseph opened the storehouses and sold supplies to the Egyptians coming for help. The famine was so bad that it spread to other regions as well, and soon the whole world was lining up to buy food from Joseph. (Genesis 41:14-57; author's retelling)

Joseph's gift brings him personal advancement, and he rises quickly to be second in command to the pharaoh. His movement is upward in vocational status and outward toward his family and community. Some would say this is typical of so-called male "phallic" movement. I'm not sure I put much stock in such language, but men do participate in the creation of families, and they create and produce things at work. It is a constructive energy not a destructive one, as the warrior imagery often implies.

For Joseph, this outward movement starts from the depths of the darkness of prison. We could see this as symbolic of adult male life that begins alone but grows outward in the building of family and career. The spirituality of building is part and parcel of this aspect of male life. The builder metaphor describes this constructive movement of men's spirituality.

Unfortunately sometimes this outward generative movement is without reflection and depth. When the outward building life is unaccompanied by inward reflection, men's lives can go awry. My hope is that men will see this building imagery as inherently spiritual as the more inward metaphors, but a building spirituality without grounding and inward depth ultimately ends up empty or even dangerous to the self and others.

This lengthy narrative about Joseph's rise from the dungeon depths to the heights of political influence offers us an opportunity to explore a variety of aspects related to male spirituality: marriage, children, career or work, money, power, and competition. Each of these areas comes out of the builder metaphor; they are aspects of building the exterior male life and at the same time aspects of the spiritual life.

Marriage

Only a very short line in the book of Genesis tells of Joseph's marriage to Asenath, the daughter of an Egyptian priest. It was a mixed marriage and an arranged marriage, which was probably ordinary in its historical and cultural context. We have already explored sexuality as a metaphor for male spirituality, but now let's look at marriage as part of being a spiritual builder.

Marriage is not part of the spirituality of every man, but it is for the majority. Most of us live out our spirituality in marriages. Marriage is about building a life together. Contrary to what John Eldredge claims,[1] I'm one man who has never dreamt about saving a princess. Instead, I always wanted to be rescued by a beautiful woman. And I was, and then she even married me!

> *Most of us live out our spirituality in marriages. Marriage is about building a life together.*

Women and men meet and love each other and get married. Healthy marriages are always a completely mutual affair in which the partners give themselves to each other. Healthy marriages are not built on one partner rescuing the other. Ernest Boyer Jr. writes,

> Marriage is the most remarkable and most courageous of all human acts—the promise of two human beings to share life together on all levels, physical, economic, spiritual—a promise made in the face of the certainty of death, the certainty of change, and the uncertainty of everything else. There is nothing else a human being might choose to do that is quite like this act, nothing so foolish or so profound.[2]

Marriage is about daily, ordinary life together, its joys and sorrows, pain and pleasure. Greeting each other with bad breath in the morning, giving each other space to wake up, preparing food, eating together, heading our separate ways for work or working together, cleaning the house, tilling the soil, pulling weeds, buying provisions, managing finances, making plans and decisions, gathering with friends, meeting the neighbors, arguing, resolving conflicts, sharing a whole spectrum of emotions, drinking a glass of wine in the evening, watching the news, making love, falling into bed tired, sleeping together. These are all ordinary marital activities, but they are also deeply spiritual as we recognize their transcendence and meaning.

Marriage is about daily, ordinary life together, its joys and sorrows, pain and pleasure.

Children

The good years in Egypt were fertile not only for the crops but also for Joseph's marriage to Asenath, which yielded him two sons. The two boys' given names are significant, as names always were in the Hebrew culture. They signify the life that Joseph is building. Manasseh (forget), the first-born, is symbolic of beginning a new life. With this new start, Joseph wants to forget the hardships of the past. He names his second son Ephraim (double blessing) because of all the prosperity he now has. The act of naming our children gives them an identity apart from us and helps them become who they are.

The act of naming our children gives them an identity apart from us and helps them become who they are.

Loving our children is a spiritual activity. Just as we have a primary need for God, we also have a second need to love and care for others. Parenthood is an expression of this need.

How is parenthood a unique expression of spirituality for fathers? I already touched on the importance of fathering earlier, in chapters 4 and 6. My purpose here is not to give helpful hints about how to be a good father but to help men understand that being a father is an expression of their spirituality. Our children will know that God loves them when they are assured that we love them. That is the depth of spirituality as a father. Father love does not control children but sacrifices on their behalf.[3] Each father will express love differently, appropriate to who he is and who his children are becoming.

> *Our children will know that God loves them when they are assured that we love them. That is the depth of spirituality as a father.*

The spirituality of fathering moves from holding to letting go.[4] I remember very clearly the birth of our children and the first emotionally charged moment of holding a tiny new human being in my hands—a human being who was conceived from the union of love between my wife and me, and who was only a few minutes earlier literally attached to her. Now I am holding this new person! "It's a miracle!" is probably the first utterance of almost every father who witnesses the birth of his child. Nineteen years after the birth of our first child, I am loving by letting go of my eldest son as he moves to another city for work. We have experienced together the rituals of initiation into manhood and now it is time to let go. This kind of love is more difficult than when I first held his fragile self in my hands. Yet I trust that God's love will now hold him in ways other than with my hands under him or my arms around him.

Work

God ordained that people should work. Adam was placed in the garden to work it and care for it (see Genesis 2:15). Work is not part of the curse, as some have surmised. But

Work is an intrinsically good and spiritual activity, not just the menial means to an end.

with the curse, both giving birth and working to feed the family become painful processes (see 3:17-19).

Work is an intrinsically good and spiritual activity, not just the menial means to an end. One of the most profound lyrics about the spirituality of work proclaims that worship and work must be one.

> Worship the Lord!
> Praise the Creator, the Spirit, the Son,
> raising our hands
> in devotion to God who is one![5]

I think that the raising of the hands in the opening refrain is not only about a posture during a church service of worship; it is raising our hands in daily work, whether it is at the office or on the construction site. Work is worship.

Unfortunately the myth that work is not worship is perpetuated by the belief that "Christian service" means professional ministry, such as being a pastor or a missionary or at least working for a charitable organization. Thus this kind of work is put on a pedestal over "secular work," which is erroneously seen as primarily about making money. But to the spiritual man, no work is primarily about making money; it is all a service to God. There is no secular work, because all work is sacred for the man who is aware of God's work. Our work is participation in the work of God.

In one of my former churches, we had the practice of featuring a "missionary of the month" in the bulletin so we could remember to pray for that person. A friend of mine, who owned and operated a window and door business, insisted that he be featured one month instead of the usual "full-time missionaries." He had it right.

The members of the Mission Springs Group (see preface) lamented that the archetypes mentioned in chapter 2 did not include the farmer, the craftsman, or even the merchant. They also have it right. Being a missionary at work is not so much about mentioning Jesus in conversation but about fulfilling the vocation or calling that God has given us.

Male spirituality is a building spirituality. Sometimes the carpenter is lauded as the quintessential worker. Maybe this is because Jesus was likely a carpenter for most of his life. The builder is a good metaphor for male spirituality, but the metaphor is not restricted to those in the construction industry. In the church are opportunities to serve on committees, teach, preach, sing songs, usher, and much more. Some men shy away from these avenues of service, but give them a building project, and they are ready with a hammer. Because physical labor is often not seen as a spiritual form of service, men do not see it as a spiritual activity. But it is a small turn to see the house that is built, the field that is plowed, the administrative task that is completed, the computer program that is designed, as a holy and creative act of worship. As part of a poem by Elizabeth Barrett Browning says,

> Every common bush on fire with God
> But only those who see take off their shoes
> The rest sit and pluck blackberries[6]

Today "plucking blackberries" has taken on an electronic form, but the failure to recognize holy bushes in our daily work is the same. A builder spirituality recognizes God's presence in the "every common bush" of our vocational life.

God worked for six days at creation. Our work too is creative, whether we create a painting, a house, a road, a program, a crop, a book, a product, or perform a human service. A friend of mine, who primarily pushes papers and ideas like I do, testifies, "I have a burning desire to create, to build, to do something physical and material that I can look at and say, 'That's good.'"

Whatever our vocation or calling is, we are participating in and continuing the work of God. If we begin to recognize our work as such, it may not only transform the way we go about our tasks, but we may ourselves be transformed in the process.

> *Whatever our vocation or calling is, we are participating in and continuing the work of God.*

That is spiritual formation. As another friend has said, "Building houses is a spiritual activity? I've never thought of it that way before. Maybe if I did I could think of myself as a spiritual person, which I've never done either." Exactly.

Panentheism is the idea that God is recognizable in all creation. I subscribe to this idea. It is not the same as pantheism, the belief that everyone and everything is divine. We recognize the divine presence not only in creation but also in our own creativity, our work. I wrote the following poem on an ordinary "day off" at home. It was only later that I discovered the word *panentheism* to describe my experience.

I think I'm a panentheist
because today I met God
in my children playing
in the dishwater (and in the clean dishes!)
in a shared meal with my friends
in a high flying kite
in the tree in the backyard
in the garden growing
in the changing of a dirty diaper
in renewed health
in a phone call from my lover
in pleasant "coincidences"
in the quiet evening sunshine
in the chirping birds
in my thoughts
in the silence
in the laughter
in the tears
in the ordinary moments of this day

Whatever the calling of a man's life is, there is the possibility of connecting with God through the ordinary moments of his work. There are a-ha moments or "God moments" when we feel completely fulfilled in the task we are called to do. I have had these on a day working at home and in the midst of a lecture or a theological discussion. My friend who is involved in construction has them when he completes a job well and views the finished product. A college athlete describes this kind of moment during a hockey game when he skates, shoots, and makes a good play.

God's name need not be uttered in praise; it may be a silent wave of emotion, but it is also that deep, spiritual sense that we are being who God has called us to be and doing what God has called us to do, whatever that is. It is recognizing God's presence in the nitty-gritty of our daily work.

Money

The bottom line of spiritual work is not about making money but about participating in God's creativity. It was probably much easier a generation or two ago, when men's work was primarily about making things instead of making money. Money is really nothing, a no thing, an illusion.[7] When money becomes the bottom line of our work, we lose all connection to the creativity of our work and the sacredness of our relationships. Even people like me in religious vocations need to be reminded of this, because working with people can also become "just a job."

When money becomes the bottom line of our work, we lose all connection to the creativity of our work and the sacredness of our relationships.

Building or creating something is directed outward, but making money is often "directed inward toward self-image, personal security, personal power and private satisfaction," says Richard Rohr.[8] It can be directed outward to pay the bills and provide for the family but also to contribute to the lives of others and to leave a personal legacy.

Jesus' favorite topic is money. There are more verses about money in the Gospels than about prayer, private Bible reading, or singing during a worship service. Our approach to money says a lot about our spirituality.

Both Jesus and money demand our allegiance; we have to choose one or the other. If we value money as the bottom line, it becomes our god. If Jesus is our God, the bottom line becomes our creative participation in the work of God's kingdom, and we value people and relationships, not possessions (see Matthew 6:19-34). We must remind ourselves that God's work is not only about missions and evangelism; it is about the redemption of all creation. Painting a picture, picking up garbage, planting a garden, teaching a child, and building a house are all part of this. Joseph's work as an administrator in the growing, harvesting, and distribution of food is also a good example.

Power

Within a relatively short time, Joseph rose from the depths of the dungeon to the heights of political power. I'm not convinced that he always dealt with his power in a healthy way. It seems he may have initially used his position to toy with his unsuspecting brothers. When the famine became severe, Joseph developed a grand scheme to feed everyone equally. This scheme almost seems like enslavement (see Genesis 47:13-26). Since we are not using Joseph as a model, we will leave these questions unanswered, even though they may trouble us. Joseph's rapid rise to power certainly does alert us to the issue of male power.

Power is not necessarily a bad thing; in fact, it is a good thing. As Leonard Beechy writes in *The Meaning of Wealth*,

"Power is the ability to get things done."[9] Power is necessary to build a marriage, a family, a house, a business, or a nation. Power is a gift that is meant to be shared, but it is very dangerous when it is hoarded and abused by men. Sometimes when men feel their power waning, they lash out and hurt those who are less powerful and therefore vulnerable.

Power is necessary to build a marriage, a family, a house, a business, or a nation. Power is a gift that is meant to be shared, but it is very dangerous when it is hoarded and abused by men.

I've never had a promotion within an organization or company, but my role as a youth pastor and now as a college professor comes with a lot of power. I'm a powerful man because I am an educated, middle-aged, white male in North America. We are the most powerful people group on the planet. This is a reality that needs to be treated with care.

Jesus also had power, all the power of heaven and earth. And his spirituality of power is instructive for us as men. When the disciples have an argument about power and influence, Jesus gives them an apt answer: "When godless rulers get power, it goes to their heads, and they throw their weight around. They use it to dominate and control others. But I want you to be different. Use your power to empower others, to serve others. That's what I came to do" (Mark 10:41-45, paraphrased). Jesus displayed this power ultimately in the cross and the resurrection. Being a servant "does not mean giving up our talent, drive, and energy. Rather, it means to place our own talent, drive, and energy completely in the service of empowering someone else."[10]

There is a little-known story from the fourth century about a monk by the name of Telemachus. The story illustrates this kind of power.[11] It was the time when gladiatorial games were popular in Roman Empire. Many Christians were opposed to this violence for entertainment. Telemachus prayed and wondered what he as one man could do about it. He decided to attend the games and found the crowds mad with excitement over the impending bloodbath. When the two gladiators faced off, Telemachus could not bear to watch and impulsively rushed between them with a wooden cross, crying out, "In the name of our Master, stop fighting!" The crowds were so incensed that they mobbed the stadium and mercilessly beat Telemachus to death. Suddenly there was a collective revulsion at what they had done, and they marched out in hushed horror. The emperor was so moved that he made an edict ending gladiatorial games. What a display of power by one little man!

The way of peace and self-sacrifice is the way of power. Jesus laid down his life on the cross and overpowered death in the resurrection. Both the cross and the resurrection are nonviolent displays of power. If we believe that the resurrection of Jesus is true, then we believe that ultimate power is nonviolent.[12] Throughout history, men have been under the illusion that the ultimate power is violence or the threat of death. Men have fought wars and ruled empires grounded in this falsehood. On the contrary, violence is always a sign of weakness.

The way of peace and self-sacrifice is the way of power. Jesus laid down his life on the cross and overpowered death in the resurrection.

Will men have the courage to wield the Jesus and Telemachus kind of power in the service of building God's household? This calls for a huge paradigm shift in how men view strength and power. It is a spirituality of power that is relational and life-giving rather than self-serving and destructive.

Competition

We have no record of Joseph engaging in chariot races or whatever form of sport was popular in ancient Egypt. But the subject of power does raise some questions about competition and sports. Women also play and watch sports, but it has been primarily a man's domain.[13] Grown men lose their cool over sports as if they were of ultimate importance. Why do competitive sports get guys going?

At coffee break in our staff lounge, men are often engaged in animated conversations about the hockey pool or the basketball playoffs. As a young man, playing tackle football without equipment was a primary way to express my masculinity. When I watch or talk about or play sports, I do it with a passion that sometimes exceeds my body's ability to handle it. The aim is always to build a champion, whether it's a round of golf, a hockey pool, or a sandlot ball game. What does competition build for men? Is there a spirituality of competition?

Competition, like power, is not necessarily about domination and defeat of the opponent. J. Denny Weaver, most known for his writing and teaching of peace theology, is also a huge sports fan and has been a competitive athlete. He writes,

> Competitive sports are explicitly cooperative endeavors. That cooperation is significant, since higher levels of achievement come only through the spur of competitive play. Thus opponents are

actually assisting each other to improve their level of play, with each athlete pushing the other to his or her highest level. Competition requires and assumes real cooperation.[14]

If winning is an end in itself, if there is intent to injure, or if the opponent is dehumanized, competition can be harmful. But it need not be that way. Even highly physical sports that involve checking, tackling, or grappling can be ways to build our bodily selves, express our physicality in a healthy and self-controlled way, and even help our competitors. Men are whole creatures, and the unpredictability, physical exertion, and sheer enjoyment of competitive sports can be a healthy expression of our spirituality.

If winning is an end in itself, if there is intent to injure, or if the opponent is dehumanized, competition can be harmful. But it need not be that way.

Sabbath

I have explored various and sundry topics under the metaphor of the builder. This chapter seems unfinished because so much more could be said about each one. Maybe this is a reminder that spiritual building is never complete. Men build marriages, families, careers, bank accounts, sports teams, and power. These are examples of the outward, generative movement of male spirituality. Male spirituality wants to create, produce, move, and build something. The key is not to label this as inherently unspiritual but to recognize God within these movements and to share them with others. Taking a Sabbath is a way to rest from and to reflect on our building work.

Money, sex, and power have been the downfall of many men because they did not know about or practice the principle of Sabbath rest. Creator God worked six days and rested on the seventh; as a result, God instituted the fourth commandment (see Exodus 20:8-11). The commandment to rest has an additional purpose, given in Deuteronomy: the Sabbath is to remember the release from enslavement in Egypt (see 5:12-15).

Taking a Sabbath is a way to rest from and to reflect on our building work.

We have become enslaved by the Egypts of workaholism, profit, and consumerism. Work is good, but even good things can consume and enslave us. Men can slide into addiction and immorality when they don't take the time to rest, reflect, and achieve depth. Sabbath is that rest and reflection.

Sabbath is literally doing nothing, a cessation of activity, but it is more than just taking a day off of work. Sabbath gives us time to reflect and to put life and work in perspective. Keeping Sabbath is a mindset of stepping back from an over-focus on work and generativity, and living contentedly in God's provision. For six days God created, but on the seventh, God rested or recreated.

Sabbath recreation might involve playing, worshipping, or even sleeping. It is different for different men. For me, because my job primarily involves things like thinking, reading, talking, and writing, I like to go in the backyard to do some physical, mindless work, like trimming trees or digging dirt, to help me recreate and refresh on a Sabbath day. That's also why I appreciate sensual rituals and times of silence during a worship service. The timing or activity is not the most important thing about Sabbath; it is just doing it, or more accurately, not doing anything that resembles our "working" days.

The purpose of the Sabbath is to rest from our work, but also to remember and reflect. The Sunday morning worship service has been a part of Christian practice for two millennia (see Acts 20:7). It is a way

Church attendance is not the only way to remember and reflect on our work and God's work, but it is a tangible, communal opportunity to do so.

to remember and reflect on the work of God in Christ. Yet indications are that church attendance is on the decline for men.[15] Church attendance is not the only way to remember and reflect on our work and God's work, but it is a tangible, communal opportunity to do so. The rest and the reflection during this day and hour are symbolic of the work of Christ on our behalf and are a taste of our eternal salvation (see Hebrews 4:1-11).

Part of the spirituality of building is to let the project sit idle for a time. It reminds us that it really doesn't depend on us, but on God, the Master Builder.

11

REFLECTION

When Jacob heard that there was food in Egypt, he said to his sons, "Why do you sit around here looking at each other, wondering what to do? Why don't you go down to Egypt and buy some food so we don't all starve to death?"

The ten oldest brothers set off to Egypt to buy food. Jacob didn't allow Benjamin to go with them, because he was afraid something bad might happen to him. He had already lost one of Rachel's sons, and he wasn't about to lose another. So the brothers joined the many others who were traveling to Egypt; they weren't the only ones hit hard by the famine.

Joseph was overseeing the distribution of food in Egypt. When his brothers arrived, they bowed down and treated him like royalty (which he was). Joseph recognized them almost immediately, but he treated them as if they were foreigners he had never seen before and spoke harshly to them, "Where are you from?"

"From Canaan," they said. "We've come here to buy food." (They obviously didn't know who he was, because they thought he was dead.)

All of Joseph's childhood memories flooded back, and he remembered his dreams and how his brothers had treated him as a result. "That's what everybody says. I think you're spies who have come to see where Egypt's weak spots are!"

"No, master," they insisted. "We've only come to buy food for our family back home. We wouldn't even think of spying!"

Joseph continued to play his game. "No, you're spies. It's written all over your faces."

The brothers were getting scared. "No, Your Highness, please believe us. We left our father and younger brother at home in Canaan, and we lost one brother years ago. All we want is food for them. This is the truth."

Joseph began to bargain. "Okay, I'll cut you a deal, since I'm a God-fearing and compassionate man. If you're as honest as you say, one of the brothers will stay here in jail while the rest of you take some grain back to your hungry families. But you have to bring your younger brother back to prove that you are telling the truth. Then I'll let you live." They agreed.

Then they started talking among themselves in Hebrew. "Now we're paying for what we did to Joseph. Remember how scared he was when we threw him into the pit? Now it's all coming back to haunt us. This is God's punishment."

Joseph had been using an interpreter, so they did not realize that he could understand every word. He could no longer keep up his hard exterior, and he turned away from them and cried. These were his brothers! When he regained his composure and could speak to them again, he tied up Simeon and had him put in jail.

Joseph then ordered that their sacks be filled with grain, that their money be put back in each sack, and that they be given provisions for the journey. This was all done for them. The brothers loaded everything on their donkeys and set off for home.

Along the way, one brother discovered that his silver had been returned and not kept as payment. Once home, the brothers all emptied their sacks—and each brother found his bag of money in his sack. There was a collective sigh of anguish and confusion. "What's going on? What's God trying to say to us?"

Jacob was visibly upset when they told him about their experience. "My life is ruined. Everything I cherish is disappearing. Joseph is gone, Simeon's gone, and now you want to take Benjamin too? If we do as you suggest, I'll be left with nothing."

The famine dragged on and just got worse. When they had finished all the food they had brought from Egypt, their father told them to go back and buy more food.

But Judah reminded him, "The man there was serious when he said, 'You won't even get a hearing if you do not have your brother with you.' So please let us take Benjamin. If you're not ready to let him go, there's no point in us going down there to buy more food."

Jacob whined in exasperation, "Why are you making my life so difficult? Why did you ever tell the man you had another brother?"

They replied in chorus, "He pressed us hard and asked pointed questions about our family: 'Is your father alive? Do you have other brothers?' We just answered honestly. How were we to know that he would tell us to bring him with us next time?"

"If it has to be, it has to be," Jacob finally said. "Take along some gifts and all the money we have,

> so you can pay back double what was returned.
> Hopefully it was just a mistake. Take your younger
> brother and be on your way. Go back to that man,
> and may the strong God give you favor in his eyes so
> that both Simeon and Benjamin will return with you.
> I have nothing else to live for. (Genesis 42:1–43:14;
> author's retelling)

The story of the uncomfortable exchange between Joseph
and his brothers and the brothers' subsequent trip home
to their father is lengthy and sometimes perplexing. All the
old memories are brought back, not only to Joseph but
also to his brothers and his father. They all share this haunting look back at the past.

The hard look back—reflecting on the past—is a powerful metaphor for men's spirituality. Although this chapter
will focus on midlife, reflection on life experiences is always
a valuable thing, regardless of our stage of life. Reflecting
on our experiences deepens our spirituality.

The "Soulscape" of Looking Back

We in the western world have plenty of opportunity to
reflect on life, because we are not consumed with simply
surviving. At midlife, we are just as close to our death as
we are to our birth. For the first time, we have as much to
look back on as we do to look forward to. That does something profound to the soul. It can kill us, or it can rebirth
us. There is great potential in this stage of life for men.

Men sometimes miss the spiritual potential of transitions
such as midlife by focusing on exterior activities, such as driv-
ing a sports car or falling into harmful activities such as workaholism or an extramarital affair. We make jokes about the

physical aspects of aging: the bulging middle, the graying or loss of hair, the waning sexual libido. May we also embrace this and every stage of life as an opportunity for growth.

Nature provides us with many analogies for spirituality. I call it the "geography of the soul" when certain landscapes illustrate spiritual realities. This past summer, our family took a hike in the Alberta Badlands near Drumheller. The distinct

At midlife, we are just as close to our death as we are to our birth. For the first time, we have as much to look back on as we do to look forward to. That does something profound to the soul.

layers of exposed soil and stone reminded me of reflecting on the various layers of life experience.

Layers of Life

The vast proud surface
lush and green
suddenly confronted by the layers
underneath
dry and ancient
even desolate
yet very much a part of me

Every layer tells a story of
a different hue
from coal black to drug white
some resistant to erosion
other layers crumble with weather
and time beyond recognition
leaving deep cross-cutting scars
transforming
with every storm

Some layers when exposed
yield fossils of a former life
barely known
scattered jigsaw pieces
put together
unfold a story
a prequel to my present

Almost a paleontologist's adventure
running with child-like glee
the panoramic peaks
pools of water at the depths
with endless layers in between

There is a certain disconcerting hesitation
to linger here too long
among the layers
yet simultaneously
a reassuring reminder
that life is deeper
than what appears
on the surface

There are all kinds of layers. The opportunity to reflect on the past as well as dream of the future can be pleasant, but it can also be difficult. Sometimes when we look back we see the vigor of youth and all our accomplishments; then we look at the present and wonder if there is anything there. Other layers remind us of past sins or pain.

An authentic spiritual life must be mined deep from our souls through the process of reflection. No matter how desolate our spirituality seems, there is life within us. It may be a deeper life that is not as visible, and we need to dig deep to discover and appreciate it. The following analogy comes from my experience of Fisherville, a ghost town of the gold rush in the interior of British Columbia.

Ghost Town

"There was once gold in them thar hills,"
bustling, booming alive with thrills.
New discoveries—
"I stake my claim!"
Struck it rich,
a life-filled vein.

But now as I walk through the silent trees,
All I feel is a hot dead breeze.
Piles and mounds,
rocks and stones,
a dry ditch,
burnt out shells
of buildings, twisted
rusty metal,
rotting flumes.

A trail once four feet now only two.
A water once golden now only blue.
Just lisping leaves,
snattering squirrels
and birds,
bugs,
historical markers,
graves.

In my mind
there is still gold,
there is still life,
but it must be mined
deep
from the earth.

The Pain of Looking Back

The look back, the mining within, can be painful and troubling. This is part of the male journey: to look at the failures, traumas, and wanderings of your past, to look again at your "previous life." This reflection is unavoidable, because only by looking inside in the midst of your exterior building life can you become a man of depth. The metaphor of reflection, which is inward, complements the outward builder metaphor. Sometimes men avoid the inward look by focusing too much on building, but both are necessary for a healthy spirituality.

Sometimes men avoid the inward look by focusing too much on building, but both are necessary for a healthy spirituality.

Joseph and his brothers must turn inward and face the trauma of their past. It was obviously a troubling look back for both Joseph and his brothers. All of them were probably content to leave the past in the past and to move on, but it was not to be. Some of the painful realities had never been dealt with. There had never been healing. A review of the past was necessary for growth in the future.

It was the same for me. In my mid-thirties I went to a spiritual director to get help for the spiritual stream that had run dry within me. I was expecting some accountability for my spiritual disciplines or some advice on how to pray better. Instead, I was led to the mirror of my soul to look at myself and the wounds of my past. Up to that point I had not reflected much on my past. I was still looking toward my future. But my first visit to a spiritual director started me on the journey toward my first significant reflection on the past. The trickle of living water on my spiritual streambed did not come as I expected.

It was very difficult for me to look back and feel the pain, fear, and betrayal of childhood abuse. However, the most difficult road for victims of abuse is the path through anger. I found it very hard to feel anger. But for real healing to happen I had to leave the role of the victim that had become my retreat during youth and young adulthood. The silence of the evil tomb of abuse had to be broken. A personal confrontation opened the way for the process of forgiveness and reconciliation.[1] The "lost boy" was found as a man, free and alive.

Part of my becoming a spiritual man was recovering my boyhood innocence. The vision of the prophet Malachi became very personal to me: "The sun of righteousness will rise with healing in its wings. And you will go out and leap like calves released from the stall" (4:2). As one who had worked on a farm where calves were kept in a dark barn until they were let out in the spring, the picture became real in my soul.

Lost Boy

Lost boy,
a wounded boy
locked up in a long winter

trying to be a man, waiting
for the sun to rise
with healing
in its Mother Hen wings . . .

Lost Boy, Found

The sun has arisen
with spring in its wing.
The calf has been let out of the stall;
blinded by the light,
leaping and jumping with careless abandon
and joy!

My reflection on the past meant dealing with a painful childhood experience. For other men it might be coming to terms with unrealized vocational dreams or the loss of a long-term job. Dreams of building do not always turn out as expected, or they vanish entirely. For some, reflection means mourning the loss of parents through death or a spouse through divorce. For a friend of mine, reflection on the past involved becoming reacquainted with a daughter he had fathered as a teenager and had lost touch with over the years. A variety of circumstances vault us into a period of reflection on the past.

The question for us in the present is whether we will take the time and energy to reflect on our experiences or continue to push the memories down in attempts to ignore our past. How we answer this question will have implications for our present and our future.

James Fowler has proposed the "conjunctive stage" of faith development beyond the "individuative-reflective stage" introduced in chapter 5. The faith task in this stage is to combine, unite, or integrate past—and sometimes disparate—circumstances and experiences into our present faith. Conjunctive faith is generally not possible before midlife, because only in midlife is there a storehouse of memories to work with. However, reflection on the past impacts our faith in the present, regardless of the stage of life we are in. Reflection pushes us toward spiritual growth.

Living in the Present

We might think that at some point in life all our questions will be answered and life will be easier. Instead, new questions emerge as we grow older. But we also become more content to live with the paradoxes and questions. Men have been driven to find answers and success, but sometimes all that we have built up crumbles around us, or we realize that the exterior life was not all it was cracked up to be. Life made more sense when we were younger and issues were less complex. Now it is time to embrace the paradoxes and to live the unanswered questions.

Men have been driven to find answers and success, but sometimes all that we have built up crumbles around us, or we realize that the exterior life was not all it was cracked up to be.

I believe that life is in many ways circular. We return to the dust from which we came. Earthly life begins when we emerge from the darkness and safety of our mother's womb, and it ends as we return to the darkness and safety of death, the womb of God. The Bible uses a lot of death, life, and rebirth language. For example, see Ezekiel 37:1-14; John 3:1-8; Romans 6:1-14. At death, life is reborn in another dimension.

What is death and life after death like? Life on earth is

mysterious enough, but the concept of eternal life in other dimensions is incomprehensible. Unanswered questions abound, but the foundation of faith remains. In fact, the questions can become an integral part of our life of faith.

The following poem represents some of my reflections on the past, present, and future. Life is not the way it used to be in the past, but it has provided a foundation for my present and future.

The Ruins of St. Mary's Mission

The concrete is cracked and crumbling
and not exactly level anymore

What used to be
a shapely profile
with walls and windows dressed
now is stripped and bare
but the foundation still is there

Many years ago it once had
a roof and doors
and you could go inside
now it's all open air
but the foundation still is there

In eighteen hundred sixty one
the structure had a mission
it was even dedicated to God
now stairs are left that lead to nowhere
but the foundation still is there

In its heyday
students sat in rows and regiment
to learn the Rs of life
now the grass and trees grow anywhere and
everywhere
but the foundation still is there

Now I see tombstones in the distance
with the river flowing by
It's a nice place to take a stroll

In our younger years, life was often more regulated and controlled, and we didn't have to worry about our physical health and appearance. Life in our middle years may not be so neat and tidy. Sometimes the stairs we have worked so hard to ascend seem to lead nowhere. We experience pain and loss. We have new questions. How will we face the future? Will we continue to build our exterior life, even though we find no meaning in doing so? Will we invest our life in the temporal pleasures of beaches and golf courses? How will we process and integrate the difficult and disconcerting events of our past? Will we "take a stroll" and enjoy the present moments and loved ones God gives us? How will we embrace the paradoxes—the unexplainable sufferings of the past and the unanswered questions about the future?

This chapter includes no references and notations to outside sources. It's not that there is no material on men's midlife experience (although more is needed, in my opinion) or that I know everything about it (I'm just starting to learn), but that this is the personal present for me. My temptation is to keep focusing on the future, as I've done all these years, or to endlessly dwell on the past, but the call is always to live in the present at whatever stage of life we are in. It is important to reflect on the past, but to do so for the purposes of a healthy and fulfilling present.

As we move into the second half of life, we become more aware of the reality of our death and the limitations of our mind and body. It can be depressing to look back and see life vigorous and exciting, and then to look ahead and see a crumbling body and eventually death.

A few years ago a good friend of ours died of cancer at age forty-six. This brought the reality of death close to me. There is nothing as effective as a funeral to put our lives into perspective. It helps us to take that evaluative look at our past and to make things right in the present, so that we can live fully in the future. Although there is always a fear of death as we contemplate its mystery, there is also a contentedness in realizing that, since there is nothing we can do to reverse the journey, we can savor and enjoy each moment more fully. Thus we become more alive even as our life draws closer to death.

As we move into the second half of life, we become more aware of the reality of our death and the limitations of our mind and body.

12

RECONCILIATION

The brothers wasted no time in getting down to Egypt and appearing before Joseph. When Joseph saw that they had Benjamin with them, he told his house steward, "Take these men to my house and make them feel at home. Butcher an animal and prepare a meal; they will eat with me at noon."

When Joseph got home, his brothers gave him their gifts and bowed respectfully before him. Joseph was more informal and started a conversation. "And your aging father whom you mentioned to me last time, how is he doing? Is he still alive?"

The brothers again bowed respectfully. "Yes, your honor, your servant our father is still alive and well, thank you."

Then Joseph took note of Benjamin, his own mother's son, and remarked, "And this is your youngest brother that you told me about?" He paused to collect himself. "God be gracious to you, my son."

Joseph was deeply moved at seeing his brother, so he excused himself and hurried off to another room. Once in his private room, he wept uncontrollably. After he collected himself and washed his face, he returned to them and said, "Let's eat."

The brothers were at a table, seated facing Joseph, arranged in order of age from the oldest to the youngest. When they noticed this, they looked at each other in amazement, wondering what might happen next. They were served lots of food, and Benjamin got by far the biggest portion. They all ate and drank freely.

After the meal, Joseph further instructed his servants: "Fill each of the men's bags with as much grain as they can carry, and put their money in their sacks just like last time. Then put my personal silver cup in the mouth of the youngest one's bag." The instructions were carried out.

At the first light of dawn the men were sent on their way. They were barely out of the city when Joseph called his steward and said, "Take off after them. When you catch up with them, say, 'Why are you trying to take advantage of us? My master's personal silver cup is missing. This is a crime!'" The servant caught up with them and repeated everything Joseph had said.

The brothers exclaimed in shock, "Why do you blame us? We would never do anything like that. We don't even know what you're talking about. Last time something like this happened, we brought the money back all the way from Canaan. Why would we now steal a silver cup from your master's house? Search our bags. If you find the cup on any of one of us, that one must die, and the rest of us will be your slaves."

"Very well then," the steward said, "but we don't have to go that far. Just the one who has the cup will be our slave. The rest of you can go free."

The brothers were so confident in themselves that they quickly opened their bags so the steward could search them. He searched their bags from the oldest to the youngest. When he got to Benjamin's, he found the cup.

The brothers were beside themselves in disbelief and despair. They loaded their donkeys and headed back to the city. Joseph was still at home when they got back, and they threw themselves on the ground in front of him.

Judah spoke for them. "We have nothing to say, master. We're too upset. There is no way we can prove our innocence. God must be punishing us. We're all in this together, and we all stand guilty before you, just as much as the one with the cup in his bag."

"I would never do that to all of you," said Joseph. "Only the one who stole the cup will be my slave. The rest of you can go back home."

Judah wouldn't let up. "Please, master, can I say just one more thing to you?" He proceeded to tell the whole family saga once more with increased urgency and pleading.

"Do you realize what this will do to our father? When we told him that you had insisted our younger brother come with us, he said, 'You know that Rachel only gave me two sons. One is missing and I presume ripped to pieces by some wild animal. I've never seen him since, and I still grieve. If I let you take the youngest and something happens to him, it will bring me to my grave in grief.'

"So can't you see that our father's very life is bound up with him? We beg you, don't make us go back to watch our father die in grief!"

Joseph couldn't stand it any longer. His heart was aching for his brothers and Benjamin and the aging father he hadn't seen in years. It was taking too much energy to act like an Egyptian ruler when he felt like a Hebrew brother. He yelled out to his attendants, "Get out! Everyone leave my presence!" They scurried out, leaving only Joseph and his brothers. Joseph starting sobbing so loudly that the entire Egyptian court heard him. Even Pharaoh heard about it.

"Come close to me," Joseph said to his brothers. And when they did, he told them the whole story. "I am Joseph, your brother, the one you sold into Egypt. Don't blame yourselves for doing this. God sent me here ahead of you to save your lives. I'm now second-in-command to Pharaoh, in charge of all his personal affairs and ruler of all of Egypt.

"Hurry back home to Dad and tell him the whole story. Then bring him with you and come back here as fast as possible. I'll give you a place to live where you'll have the best land and be close to me. I'll take care of everything."

The brothers were stunned and speechless.

"Take a good look at me. It's me; I'm your brother, telling you this with my own mouth. Tell Dad about my high position here and everything that has happened. Why are you just standing there? Get going!"

Then Joseph threw himself on Benjamin, hugged him, and wept. Benjamin too broke into sobbing as they embraced. Joseph hugged and kissed each of his brothers and wept over them.

The whole story reached the ears of Pharaoh. He thought this was a feel-good story: a foreign slave boy, now his right-hand man, meets up with his long-lost family.

Pharaoh told Joseph, "Tell your brothers to take

extra donkeys and supplies, load up their father and families, and bring them back here. We'll settle them in the best land in Egypt. They shouldn't worry about leaving things behind. The best of Egypt will be theirs here."

And they did just that. Joseph joked with his brothers as they left, "Take it easy on the trip. Try to get along with each other." (Genesis 43:15–45:24; author's retelling)

The long and detailed story of Joseph's brothers' visits is an amazing and emotional process of forgiveness and reconciliation. I love the passion of their relationship that finally bursts forth when Joseph reveals his identity. He can only stand to be the lone ruler for so long before he has to tell the truth and reveal his deepest need for a restored relationship with his brothers. What a beautiful model! Male maturity is more about the wisdom of building peace than about the wildness of making war.

It's always been a bit of a mystery to me why Joseph didn't reveal his identity as soon as he met his brothers. Does he find some pleasure in giving them a hard time and watching them squirm? Was this his idea of sweet revenge? Throughout the ordeal, Joseph retains his position of power. It's a position he seems to use to psychologically torment his brothers in return for their cruel treatment of him many years earlier. Or was he actually still afraid of them and merely testing the authenticity of their claims? Was he trying to find out whether they were still angry with him? The text does not answer these questions. Whatever the nuances and motivations behind the process, it is a beautiful story about the emotional vulnerability of Joseph and his brothers and about their reconciliation.

The Process of Reconciliation

Joseph's revelation of his identity and his reunion with his brothers seems to be carefully choreographed and controlled—except for the emotional outbursts. Maybe the long and deliberate process was also because of Joseph's need to control the situation, which he was not able to do as a younger man. In this process, Joseph clearly articulates what his brothers have done to him, and they feel genuine remorse at their actions. Joseph sees how God has worked for the good of all in the circumstances and offers his forgiveness. The foundation for reconciliation has been laid.

The process of reconciliation is exactly that—a process. It does not happen automatically, quickly, or easily.

The process of reconciliation is exactly that—a process. It does not happen automatically, quickly, or easily. Forgiveness is closely related to reconciliation. Forgiveness is an act of the will, but it is also a process. There are layers or levels of both forgiveness and reconciliation.

I'm not sure I have experienced all of these layers, but there was at least one significant layer that was instrumental in my healing. Healing from childhood abuse does not necessarily require personal confrontation or reconciliation with the abuser, but in my case it is something I desired in order to move on in my life. I, like Joseph, had grown to be a successful man on the outside, but inside, a wound continued to fester.

Jesus came to bring healing and reconciliation to our

relationships, and as a follower of Jesus, I saw myself as a carrier of the message of the reconciliation (see 2 Corinthians 5:16-21). Reconciliation is a strong metaphor for salvation and for what it means to be Christian. I wanted this for myself and for the man who had betrayed my trust as a child.

I think it is important that a process of reconciliation includes marking events or symbolic rituals. For me, this event involved a meeting for confrontation, apology, forgiveness, and a degree of reconciliation. Sometimes we have the idea that spontaneous acts are more genuine than planned ones, but that is not necessarily so. Meetings laden with significance and with the possibility of deep emotional expression usually go better if there is careful thought and planning. It was very important for me, as a victim who was not in control when the abuse happened, to be in control of the planning of such an event.

Reconciliation is a strong metaphor for salvation and for what it means to be Christian.

My meeting of reconciliation included a statement I wrote about what I had experienced, his apology and acknowledgment of hurt, and my assurance of forgiveness. Both of us were honest and genuine in our statements. It was also important that support people each of us had chosen were present to witness our words and actions. The meeting also included a "relief activity" that symbolized forgiveness and reconciliation: we played a game of football that was a reminder of the positive contribution he had made to my life despite the pain that his acts of sexual abuse had caused.

Reconciliation does not mean that things will be as they

were before the wrong occurred. I will never again be this man's little buddy, and he will never again be my hero and mentor. Geographical moves and vocational paths had already separated us when I reached adulthood. The important thing for me now is that he no longer holds

Reconciliation does not mean that things will be as they were before the wrong occurred.

unconscious power over me, and I hold no animosity or anger toward him. I am free, and I pray for him in his own journey. I do not deny that he hurt and betrayed me. But with forgiveness I can also honor him as one who mentored me in positive ways.

Reconciliation is a powerful metaphor for male spirituality. My example is very personal, but reconciliation is the same on international levels as it is on personal ones.

The Peace-Builder

In the archetypal system, the warrior is the primary symbol of male spirituality, but I would propose that the peace-builder become the primary motif. Who are the strong spiritual men of history? In the old system it was kings, princes, presidents, and military heroes. It was men who would fight for a cause with the same or greater violent tenacity as the enemy.

I would propose that the peace-builders who have given their lives by waging peace are the real spiritual men—Mahatma Gandhi, Martin Luther King Jr., and Nelson Mandela, to name a few well-known men. Tom Fox is another. He was one of four members of Christian Peacemaker Teams who was kidnapped in Iraq in late 2005. He died for the cause of reconciliation between Iraq and his country, the United States.[1]

It is good to have peace-builder heroes, but it is the millions of nameless men like you and me who reconcile with their brothers, who reach out to their children, who make friends with the stranger, who will be transformed, and who will transform this warring world. Peace-builders do not sit back in fear and passivity and let injustice happen. They respond with the courageous power of love.

Peace-builders do not sit back in fear and passivity and let injustice happen. They respond with the courageous power of love.

The response to injustice requires activity. The warrior and the peace-builder are often motivated to act by the same thing, albeit in different ways. It is the same motivation that propelled me toward personal healing and reconciliation. It is an unlikely thing, one that men struggle with deeply and widely. It is anger.

In my background, anger was suspect of being sin, but the Bible says only that when we are angry, we should not sin (see Ephesians 4:26). Of course, anger has caused men to sin in grievous and deadly ways, so caution and reflection are essential guardrails. But anger can be a positive emotion if it is processed and expressed in constructive ways.

For example, Jesus was angry when the temple was desecrated, and he did something about it (see Mark 11:15-17). A visualization of this story was instrumental in my healing journey from abuse. My counselor asked me, "Your body is a temple of the Holy Spirit. How do you think Jesus would have responded to the desecration of your body?" and she invited me to respond, not by seeking vengeance on the perpetrator, but by seeing the injustice as Jesus would see it. Anger at injustice is appropriate and goads us to action. It finally got me out of my victim's shell toward healing and reconciliation. Anger is a powerful male emotion that often gets the better of us and turns into rage. But rather than suppressing it, let us harness anger in the service of building peace.

Male Emotions

Joseph's emotional vulnerability finally propels what had been beneath the surface to the forefront. His emotional expression can be a model for all men. From Robert Bly's *Iron John* to the Promise Keepers' mass rallies to contemporary young men who are much more comfortable than their fathers with showing emotion—the men's movement in its varied forms has done well in getting men more in touch with their emotions.

This is difficult to reconcile with the emphasis on the warrior archetype. A soldier's job is to kill the enemy. To kill, it helps to be emotionless and detached from the other, the enemy.[2] No normal man in his right mind could be fully emotionally engaged and kill a fellow human being after looking the other in the eye, unless that emotion was extreme rage. A peace-builder's job is to reconcile with the enemy. For reconciliation, it helps to be emotionally open and empathetic to the other, the enemy.

Do real men cry? Of course they do! Men have sometimes been taught that it is "sissy" to cry or show emotion, but it takes a real man to be honest and open about a feeling, whether it is agony or ecstasy. Fathers often teach their sons to be tough and strong, to "take it like a man." Sometimes when doubts, fears, or sufferings come, crying is the appropriate emotion. Real men do cry.[3]

Too often men's interaction is on a surface level. We talk about sports in a bar after a few beers to relax us. We go hunting or fishing or golfing, where talking can be bad etiquette. But what we need is connection on a deeper emotional level. That is not only what women want and need but also what we need from each other as men.

When our Mission Springs Group met every month, we didn't talk much about sports or politics or work, but about our relationships with our fathers, wives, children, and God, and how all those are related. We talked about what was going on beneath the surface: our feelings, doubts, questions, and fears. We talked about what matters. There was lots of laughter, but there was also heartache, frustration, and compassion. The meetings gave us a new structured opportunity for emotional depth and spiritual vulnerability. Relationships with our wives, children, friends, and colleagues—and our relationships in the world at large—are hopefully better because of our emotional vulnerability with each other.

Male Friendship

Although the story of Joseph does not mention male friendships outside the family, the metaphor of reconciliation leads us to talk about male friendship. Reconciliation involves emotional vulnerability, and so does friendship. Reconciliation is about restored relationships. We cultivate those relationships through ongoing friendships. Spirituality as friendship might also be a stretch for many men, but Jesus

Spirituality as friendship might also be a stretch for many men, but Jesus calls his disciples friends. Being friends with each other also helps us to be friends with Jesus.

calls his disciples friends (see John 15:15). Being friends with each other also helps us to be friends with Jesus.

The best example of biblical male friendship is between two young warriors who by all indications should have been enemies or at least competitors: Jonathan and David. The account of their friendship in 1 Samuel 18–20 includes a number of detailed descriptions of the depth of their relationship, for example, "The soul of Jonathan was knit to the soul of David, and Jonathan loved him as his own soul" (1 Samuel 18:1 NKJV).

Although David kills his tens of thousand in battle, their military exploits do not seem to be important in their friendship. They are soul friends. Their friendship is even bound together with a covenant that preserves their friendship through trying times (see 18:3; 20:4). Jonathan is the rightful heir to the throne, but he advocates for David and protects him from his father's murderous rampages (see 19:1-7; 20:26-42). Friendship becomes David's salvation. Years later, after Jonathan is dead and David is king, David remembers his covenant with Jonathan and shows kindness to Jonathan's disabled son, Mephibosheth (see 2 Samuel 9). Depth, emotional vulnerability, and loyalty mark this friendship. Male friendships are not only our salvation; they are part of our male spirituality.

I have a best friend. We have been friends since we were kids. We grew up in the same community and church youth group, although it was not until we had both graduated from high school that the two of us became close friends. We worked at camp together and went to the same Bible college, but then married women who had never met each other. They couldn't help but become friends! When they became pregnant around the same time and gave birth to firstborn sons within a few weeks of each other, their friendship took off, and the friendship that the two of us men shared deepened another level.

We took holidays together and spent a lot of time together as families in subsequent years. When we lived in the same city, we met for breakfast once a week. Now, whenever we meet, we continue where we left off, whether it's jabbing each other with creative insults, sharing deep pain, or dreaming together about future possibilities. We know where the other is coming from, and we trust each other with who we are. We don't have to beat around the bush to find out the truth. Every year my friend comes out for a week of hiking and conversation. It's good to have him as a friend.

Friendship

We intimate with words
blasphemies
heart cries
    frustrations
        (money, sex and lack of power)
    ordinarities
        (God and politics
        sins of fathers
        hopes for sons and daughters
        love)
    occasional vulgarities
    but few trivialities
and our spirits holy kiss
our souls embrace
    real
    and deep

Relational Spirituality

Reconciliation, emotional vulnerability, and human friendship are all related to how we think about God. How we think about God has a lot to do with how we live and relate in our everyday lives. How we conceive of God and how God works with humanity and the world is the subject of countless thick and heavy volumes throughout history. I won't pretend to solve the riddle in a few words here. All I propose is that reconciliation and self-giving love become primary metaphors for a maturing male spirituality.

How we think about God has a lot to do with how we live and relate in our everyday lives.

Salvation within evangelicalism has often been reduced to personally "accepting Jesus into your heart." This metaphor has been part of influencing generations of North American men (and women) toward an individualistic and increasingly selfish spirituality based on self-fulfillment. The ultimate reward is "going to heaven," getting a taste of our own pie in the sky by and by when we die. But Jesus came not so much to save individual souls for life in another dimension as to proclaim the Jubilee and inaugurate a commonwealth of love and justice in the here and now. Jesus came to reconcile all things to himself (see Luke 4:14-30; Colossians 1:20). He came to fulfill God's agenda of global reconciliation that includes all people and all creation, not just individuals' personal needs.

Traditionally, Jesus' suffering and death have been seen by many as the terrible and violent punishment for sin that God would have inflicted on us had Jesus not stepped in as our substitute, thus appeasing or satisfying God's wrath.

This penal substitutionary imagery has been popularized in song lyrics, sermon illustrations, and graphically in movies like *The Passion of the Christ* (2004). But has it also inadvertently contributed to the myth of redemptive violence that has been embraced in Christendom for centuries? Powerful men in church and politics, in the past and present, have held to this myth. And young men have been asked to kill and be killed for the sake of peace and security, that is, salvation.

So, what does all this theology have to do with male spirituality? This view of God and Christ's atonement has unfortunately been the primary shaper of men's spirituality in North America. But it is only one of the numerous biblical metaphors that help us to understand the mystery of the atonement.[4] It needs to be reevaluated for us to build a more constructive spirituality, for men in particular. A relational men's spirituality begins with a reexamination of our view of God and our relationship with God, which subsequently shapes our view of ourselves as men and then our relationships with women, children, and people of other religions, cultures, and nations.

God is loving, but even stronger than that, God is love (see 1 John 4:7-12). Love is about relationship. God demonstrated the vulnerability of love in becoming human in Jesus of Nazareth. This means that it was not so much God's vengeful hatred of our sin that sent Jesus to the cross, but rather Jesus'

> *Love is about relationship. God demonstrated the vulnerability of love in becoming human in Jesus of Nazareth.*

passion for God's kingdom of love that caused the rulers of the violent kingdoms of the day to execute him.[5] Male spirituality is then about giving up control and embracing others with the powerfully transforming, self-giving, reconciling love of Christ. James Fowler says it well:

> For men, the trajectory toward moral [and spiritual] wholeness means learning to think and feel more holistically, to overcome excessive detachment, and to learn to see persons in relationships and in the context of shared histories and mutual responsibilities. It means, for men, strengthening the ability and effective care of ongoing communities and webs or relationships.[6]

Men, let's get with God's agenda and embrace a more communal spirituality in which reconciliation and friendship are the preferred metaphors for salvation and spirituality. It will have profound implications for us, for our families, and for the world. We will have more mutually respectful marriage and family relationships, and someday there may even be peace between warring nations as a result. Embracing a more communal spirituality starts with how we see God's relationship to us and becomes our model for a life that includes vulnerability, forgiveness, reconciliation, friendship, and community.

13

LEGACY

When the brothers got back home to their father in Canaan, their words stumbled over each other with excitement. "You won't believe this! Joseph is still alive—and he's ruler over all of Egypt!" Jacob went numb; he couldn't believe what he was hearing. As they repeated the story and he saw the heavily laden donkeys, his heart started beating again.

"Okay, okay, I believe you. Joseph is still alive. I must see him again before I die."

So they packed up everything and set out. At Beersheba, Jacob stopped to pray and sacrifice. He received assurance from God that this was the right thing to do. He would see Joseph again, and Joseph would be holding his hand when he died.

When Joseph got word that they were on their way, he called for his chariot, and he rushed out to Goshen to meet them. The moment he saw his father, he ran to him and threw his arms around him and wept for a long time.

Jacob comforted him and said, "Now I'm ready to die. I've looked into your face. You are indeed alive."

Joseph settled his father and brothers and their families in Egypt on the best land available in Goshen, just as Pharaoh had directed. They were all well taken care of, right down to the smallest baby.

When Jacob was about to die, he called for Joseph and said, "Give me your word that you will show kindness and faithfulness to me and our family. Do not bury me in Egypt when I die, but carry me back to rest with our ancestors." Joseph made a solemn vow to carry out his father's request.

Sometime later Joseph was told that his father was in his last days. So he took his two sons, Manasseh and Ephraim, along with him to visit Jacob. Jacob rallied his strength and sat up in bed as they arrived.

Just then he noticed the two boys with Joseph and said, "And who are these?"

Joseph told his father, "These are the sons God has given me in this place."

"Bring them closer to me so I can bless them," Jacob said. His eyesight was failing in his old age, and he was almost blind. When Joseph brought them closer, Jacob kissed and embraced them and said to Joseph, "I never even expected to see you again, and now I get to see your children as well!"

Joseph bowed respectfully and put Ephraim to Jacob's left and Manasseh on his right. But Jacob crossed his arms and put his right hand on the head of Ephraim, the younger son, and his left hand on the head of Manasseh, the firstborn. Then he blessed them.

When Joseph saw that his father had his right hand on his younger son's head, he thought he had made a mistake and corrected him, saying, "That's the wrong head, Father. The other one is the first-born. Put your right hand on his head."

But Jacob insisted. "I know exactly what I'm doing. They will both develop a people but the younger will be greater and his descendants will enrich nations."

Jacob called all his sons around him and blessed each of them. When he had finished, he pulled his feet up into his bed, breathed his last, and was gathered to his people.

Joseph supervised the embalming of Jacob's body, after which there was a period of mourning in Egypt. Joseph asked Pharaoh for permission to take his father's body back to his homeland for burial. A number of officials and dignitaries accompanied Joseph's family on the procession back to Canaan. Jacob's sons carried out all their father's wishes exactly as he had requested and buried him in the field that Abraham had bought as a burial plot.

Joseph and his whole extended family stayed in Egypt; he even saw the birth of his great-grand-children there. Joseph made his brothers promise that they would take his bones back to the land of his ancestors after he died.

Joseph died at the age of 110 years. They embalmed him and laid him in a coffin in Egypt. (Genesis 45:25–46:7; 46:28–47:12; 47:28–49:1; 49:33; 50:1-26; author's retelling)

A man's legacy is not primarily about leaving money to the next generation or leaving a reputation for the history books. It's about leaving a legacy of ongoing community that spans the generations. Ultimately Joseph's whole family moves to Egypt and is cared for there. When Joseph dies, his bones lie in state in a foreign land, but both his bones and his people eventually return home.

Jacob's blessing of Joseph's sons continues the strange

pattern set by earlier generations and foreshadows the upside-down nature of God's kingdom as inaugurated in Jesus. Abraham was a nobody out of Ur; Isaac was younger than his half-brother Ishmael; Jacob was the second twin after Esau; Joseph was eleventh in line, even if he was the firstborn of Jacob's favorite wife. The Gospels continue the theme of the unlikely righteous, with prostitutes and tax collectors being the heroes. In that light Jacob crossing his hands over Joseph's sons is not surprising. It was obviously deliberate and thematically appropriate even if culturally contradictory.

A man's legacy is not primarily about leaving money to the next generation or leaving a reputation for the history books. It's about leaving a legacy of ongoing community that spans the generations.

Christian male spirituality also sometimes goes against all the cultural norms. I have proposed that male spirituality begins with the recognition that we are the beloved. This is in contrast to a culture that says we should be the lovers, initiators, and aggressors. Men's spirituality ends in compassionate community rather than with individuation and personal fulfillment, as our culture would have us believe. Although I proposed that the metaphor of journey is more appropriate for male spirituality than the more feminine metaphor of home, Joseph's life ends with a request to take his bones back to his homeland. When people are near death, they often desire to return home to their roots. In death we return home.

A Communal Spirituality of Death

What is death like? Numerous people have had near-death experiences; some even claim to have experienced death for a time, only to return to life. I have no experience, but I do wonder about it. A beautiful night, camping in the Okanagan Valley in the interior of British Columbia with my family, brought on a rather strange wondering about death:

A Warm Summer's Night (After a Day That's Been So Right)

Is death like going to sleep
after a day that's been so right
traveling with my loved and known
arriving at our destination's height

Is death like going to sleep
on a warm summer's night
with crickets' lullaby
surrounded by the dark unknown
and God's winking starlight

Is death like going to sleep
on a warm summer's night
with the dry Okanagan breeze
blowing in Jann Arden's voice
can't make out the words
but the sound's pure delight

Is death like going to sleep
after a day that's been so right
now my eyelids doing the slow-dance down
and everything around pulling me in
to turn out the lantern
and surrender my body
to the mystery of a warm summer's night
?

Death is one of the great mysteries of life. I know very little about dying or death, but my experience that night gave me a positive and communal picture of death.

Nearly all people will or have experienced the death of a loved one, whether it is the death of a close friend, a parent, a spouse, or a child. This past year, two of my colleagues and one retired colleague died of cancer. I have also attended the funerals of grandparents and other relatives, and sometimes attended in support of my friends and colleagues who have lost a loved one. Death reminds us of the fragility and the preciousness of life. Remembrance of the dead draws the living into community.

Death reminds us of the fragility and the preciousness of life. Remembrance of the dead draws the living into community.

The closing narrative of the book of Genesis includes accounts of the deaths of Jacob and Joseph. There is very little narrative between their deaths. They both request that their bones be taken back to their homeland (see Genesis 49:29-33; 50:22-26). Although Jacob is "gathered to his people," extensively mourned over, and eventually returned to his ancestral burial place, Joseph is simply embalmed and placed in a coffin in Egypt. His bones were not returned until a few generations later (see Exodus 13:19; Joshua 24:32).

I do not believe that the spirituality of home in the face of death is accidental or euphemistic. Its terminology is rooted in the spirituality of death and dying. Death separates the dead from the living, but death invites the dead into a new community, a community in which the living are also attached. Seen this way, the relationship between death and life is more circular than linear. In death, as in God, there is no past, present, and future.

I love the phrase "gathered to his people." It is much deeper than some of our modern death language, such as "passed away" or "gone to a better place." The modern terms are geographically based, whereas the ancient Hebrew is relationally based. In death, male spirituality is a spirituality of community.

Eating alone is sad, but perhaps the greatest tragedy is to die alone. This is portrayed poignantly by the contrast between the main characters in the movie *The Bucket List*, a recent movie that contrasts two different ways to approach death. Edward Cole, a selfish billionaire played by Jack Nicholson, is tormented by the thought of dying alone. Carter Chambers, the garage mechanic played by Morgan Freeman, is surrounded by family members as he faces his death. Death, like other important life transitions, is meant to be experienced in community.

What does Jesus do in his last days? He has a meal with his closest friends. He shows them how to love deeply by washing their feet, a service usually done by a slave (see John 13:1-17). A number of my friends have described for me the last days with their loved ones dying of cancer. They tell of intimate times of family and close friends gathering together to cherish past memories, to laugh and to cry, to suck every ounce of the present out of the moments they have.

> *In times when death is knocking at the door, spending time with loved ones and expressing love becomes the highest priority.*

In times when death is knocking at the door, spending time with loved ones and expressing love becomes the highest priority. Being "gathered to our people" is then natural in our last days.

Maybe we should always live like this—not with a sense of dread or fatalism but with a sense that every moment is a gift to be shared. Why not always focus on what is most important? Jesus did nothing different in his last days than he did all his life. He was devoted to loving others. We die as we have lived. Men who have lived a spirituality of community leave a legacy of communal bonds when they die.

When Life and Death Don't Make Sense

I tend to be idealistic in my writing. It's easy to do. A book is not real life. It is only words on a page. Even Joseph's life has a happy ending. Joseph makes up with his family, everyone gets fed, and they live happily ever after in Egypt. Well, for a generation anyway, and then they become slaves, but I'm ending this book before we get to that part.

Joseph's bones do not find their final resting place until many years later, after the enslavement in Egypt, the exodus, the wandering in the wilderness, the crossing of the Jordan, and the Canaanite wars (see Joshua 24:32). That's when Joseph's bones finally come home and are gathered to his people. In that sense, the communal happy ending was somewhat delayed.

Life doesn't always make sense, even in retrospect. The questions remain unanswered and the purpose or "end" is often unclear. Does anyone see any good in global atrocities, such as genocides, or in personal tragedies, including death before old age? It is in these times that we cry out to God because these events seem to contradict God's purposes of shalom. When we don't know how to make something right or don't have the power to make something right, we lament. To lament is to sorrow over what is not as

God intended. Sometimes that is all we can do when life and death make no sense. The sage in Ecclesiastes articulates this,

> I have seen something else under the sun:
>   The race is not to the swift
>   or the battle to the strong,
>   nor does food come to the wise
>   or wealth to the brilliant
>   or favor to the learned;
>   but time and chance happen to them all.
>
> Moreover, no one knows when their hour will come:
>   As fish are caught in a cruel net,
>   or birds are taken in a snare,
>   so people are trapped by evil times
>   that fall unexpectedly upon them.
>
> As you do not know the path of the wind,
>   or how the body is formed in a mother's womb,
>   so you cannot understand the work of God,
>   the Maker of all things. (Ecclesiastes 9:11-12; 11:5)

It all sounds a bit confusing and depressing, but in death we finally acknowledge that we don't understand it all, and we entrust ourselves to God, who does. Life in the bigger picture is like the journey of Joseph's bones. The happy ending of one generation might give way to tragedy in the next or vice versa. We do not control the future, but we can entrust our lives to the One who does. We can leave a legacy of spirituality for the next generation, regardless what circumstances they might have to face.

"God works in mysterious ways" goes the old cliché. Joseph also recognized this as he reflected on his family's journey. He assured his brothers that when they planned harm for him, God used those same plans for his good and their good. God works even in the midst of transition and tragedy.

We do not control the future, but we can entrust our lives to the One who does.

People respond variously to catastrophe, but the two common poles are denial and despair. Those who live in denial refuse to see what is right before their eyes. Those who live in despair see only what is right before their eyes.[1] God sees in the eternal now the bigger picture that eludes us.

Shalom Spirituality

We are assured that God desires a "happy ending" for all people and all creation. We are also assured that God's purposes will be accomplished in Christ, even though God always gives people freedom to choose to live in God's way.[2] The eschatological promise of God is clear in the prophetic books of the Old and New Testaments. In the meantime there will be destruction and chaos. But God and God's shalom purposes will be victorious. In cynical moments I say that these only happen in the movies, but shalom experiences are very real, and they are small tastes of what God wills for us all the time. Sometimes we have the privilege of catching glimpses of this shalom.

One such taste came for me a few years ago when I was coaching one of my sons' soccer team. I had not planned on coaching. A few weeks after the season should have started, I received a desperate call that said my son, and a number of other boys, would not be able to play if they did not get a coach. As it turned out, all the other coaches had already formed their teams. So what I got was a collection of unwanted players from last year's teams plus those who were new to the community. None of the boys knew

Shalom experiences are very real, and they are small tastes of what God wills for us all the time. Sometimes we have the privilege of catching glimpses of this shalom.

each other. They were from various racial, ethnic, and language groups. And very few had soccer experience. On the surface, they seemed like a group of losers and misfits.

During the first practice I had to endure barbs of disrespect from a few players, put a stop to some racist jokes with ensuing fights, and grimace as a few boys struggled to even jog around the perimeter of the field. I said to myself at the end of the practice, "I got the Bad News Bears, and unfortunately this ain't the movies."[3]

I sat the boys down after the first practice and set some ground rules about jokes, insults, and the like. I gave them a pep talk about teamwork and mutual respect. We lost every game for the first half of the season, and we didn't win many in the second half. But I kept track of scores and encouraged the boys with the statistic that the second time around we had done better against each team we played. They had scored more goals—or their opponents had scored less. We were improving! "Feel good about yourselves!" I said.

To make a long story short, the next season continued where the first had left off. We won more games than we lost during the season, and we peaked for the playoffs.

The championship game started like the script for a movie. Our opposition arrived with matching warm-up uniforms, equipment bags, and professional preparation routines. We were the overwhelming underdogs, having lost to this team twice during the regular season.

The game also unfolded like it was scripted for a classic. We were down 0-3 after the first half, with our opposition riding a wave of confidence. But we managed to claw back to within a goal and tied the game with only minutes remaining. Nothing was settled during two periods of overtime, so the game went into a shoot-out pitting their all-star goalie against Sergei, our four-foot-nothing keeper who had a whole four games of experience in the net under his belt. It went down to the last shooter—and we won! It was one of those moments a coach and a team only dream of. In a post-game speech, I reminded the boys where we had come from two years before.

I don't want to over-spiritualize this little victory, but I believe this is what the kingdom of God is about. It is about breaking down barriers between people so we can work together for the common good. In this case, it was only a soccer trophy, but that prize illustrates the larger picture of life. God wants all of us misfits to be winners together, to experience the fullness of God's redemption and victory as a community of humankind.

Too often male spirituality has focused on self-actualization, where victory for one is defeat for another. But our enemy is never another person; it is enmity itself. Our enemy is strife, separation, and dehumanization.

Too often male spirituality has focused on self-actualization, where victory for one is defeat for another. But our enemy is never another person; it is enmity itself. Our enemy is strife, separation, and dehumanization. May we band together as a team against that enemy for the sake of ourselves and our human community. That is the best legacy men can leave for future generations.

MEN'S SPIRITUALITY UNDER CONSTRUCTION

We have explored ten metaphors for men's spirituality from the life of Joseph. These are not the only metaphors, and they do not make a complete masterpiece. Men's spirituality is still under construction. Yet I hope that these metaphors will encourage men to be and become who they are. I hope that men might say, after reading this book, "I'm more spiritual than I thought I was" or "I'm a real man after all" or "Now I'm motivated in my quest to be a spiritual man."

Men's spirituality is not so much about being a meditating monk, a wild warrior, a rescuing knight, or a conquering king. It is not so much about being the perfect Christian, the spiritual leader of the house or the godly mentor of the next generation. There is no ideal real spiritual man to try to be like or to feel guilty about not being like. Guilt is not a good motivator. Start from where you are and become who you are.

Men's spirituality reaches its height when it shows compassion to all people, beginning with those close to us. It is not about I, me, and mine. It is about us, we, and them. It is about participation in building God's commonwealth of love and justice. The individual journey becomes a communal journey of reunification. Male spirituality begins with specialness and individuation but leaves a legacy of compassionate community.

Male spirituality is about recognizing and experiencing ourselves as beloved. It is about dreaming the dreams of God's shalom for all. It is about having the courage to face the wounds of our past. It is about seeing our spirituality as an ongoing journey. It is about fidelity in our sexuality, our relationships. It is about sharing the gift of leadership with women. It is about building a marriage, a family, and a career, and empowering others to build with us. It is about accepting ourselves where we are in life, looking back and looking ahead. It is about reconciliation and friendship as the primary motifs of the spiritual life. It is about leaving a legacy of shalom community.

Men's spirituality is asking the question "What is a real spiritual man?" and then living the question. Perhaps that has been part of our problem as men: we think we must have all the answers, we think we have to be in charge and have it all together to be a "real man" who is authentically spiritual. Men's spirituality is by its very nature always under construction. As the great German poet Rainer Maria Rilke advised his young protégé:

Be patient toward all that is unsolved in your heart. And try to love the questions themselves.

Do not seek answers that cannot be given to you because you would not be able to live them.

And the point is to live everything.
Live the questions now.

Perhaps you will then gradually,
without noticing it,
live some distant day into the answer.[1]

DISCUSSION GUIDE

Although I am by nature a very systematic person, my experience of leading a discussion around the reading of this book did not involve a highly structured format. (It was good for me to be less structured. And most men don't like to be told what to talk about anyway!) The most important ingredient was that the men had read the chapter and came prepared with responses to the reading, both the Joseph story and the content of the chapter.

It is important to let men tell their stories about how they experience their relationship with God. Sometimes some thoughtful reflection and discussion about men's spirituality can help us toward action that is consistent with God's mission in the world. Your group's discussions will be personal, but they hold great import for our communities and our larger society.

I hope that the following questions will be helpful for facilitating some honest discussion about male spirituality. Feel free to add, delete, change, adapt, and use them in any order.

1. The Personal Quest

1. Share about your experience of becoming a man. When and how did you realize you were a man?

2. The author defines *spirituality* as "the quest for relation to the Other." Does the author's definition fit your understandings? Why or why not?

3. What picture or description of a spiritual man has been dominant in your life, church, or community?

4. What are your deepest desires as a man? What are your deepest fears?

5. Which aspects of the author's personal quest can you identify with? Which aspects are different for you?

2. The Quest in Literature

1. What books have you read or what meetings have you attended that explored male spirituality? What is your response to these?

2. What do you think of the four male archetypes: warrior, king, lover, wise man? Which ones do you identify with the most or the least? Why? What do you think about the addition of the farmer and/or craftsman to the list?

3. What do you think about the warrior archetype? Can you identify? Why or why not?

4. How do you respond to some of the questions and critiques raised about the warrior as a primary motif for male spirituality?

3. The Quest in the Bible

1. How do you view God? How do you feel about God being portrayed as a female as well as male? What does this discussion say about us as men? As humans?

2. Who is your favorite man in the Bible? What do you find attractive about him? What qualities do you admire?

3. What do you think of the story of Joseph? What do you like or dislike about his story and person?

4. Beloved

1. Was Joseph beloved or just spoiled? Why do you think so? What do you think of the relationships and dynamics in Jacob's family?

2. Read Luke 3:21-22 and parallels in the other Gospels. What do you think of the author's use of this text as a foundation for male spirituality?

3. How have you experienced being loved or unloved in your life?

4. What kind of relationship have you had with your father in the different stages of your life? How has this shaped who you have become?

5. How are our human relationships intertwined with our relationship with God? Why is it difficult for men to receive love from God and from people?

6. If you are a father, how do you best express love for your children? How can you make all of them your favorite?

5. Dreamer

1. What do you think of Joseph's dreams? How do you respond to all the other dreams and visions in the Bible?

2. Read Isaiah 2:2-4; 11:6-9. What are God's dreams for the world and the human race? How does this dream affect men's spirituality?

3. How were dreams defined in the chapter? What is your experience with different types of dreams?

4. Are dreams and visions still relevant today? How do we interpret them?

5. What were your dreams as a boy and/or as a young adult? How do you view those today?

6. Wounded

1. How do you think Joseph felt toward his brothers before and after the incident in the field?

2. Read 2 Corinthians 12:7-10. Why is it difficult for men to admit weakness, struggle, pain, dependence? What is good about admitting these?

3. Have you experienced childhood wounding? How has this affected and shaped who you have become?

4. Why is the "father wound" experienced by many men so deeply? How might it influence male spirituality?

5. How do you process wounds, pain, or suffering in your life?

7. Journey

1. What changes and what stays the same for Joseph after his journey to Egypt?

2. Read Philippians 3:12-16. Compare Paul's description of the spiritual journey with Joseph's geographical and spiritual journey. How is your faith journey similar to and/or different from these? How is your faith journey similar to and/or different from other men in the Bible, such as Jacob or Moses?

3. Share personal stories of both geographical and spiritual journeys during young adulthood.

4. Share stories of geographical moves, recreational journeys, or religious pilgrimages. How have these shaped your spirituality?

5. Which of the poems can you relate to best: "Goodbye/Hello" or "In Golden"? Why?

6. Have you found contentment where you are at present in your spiritual life? What is it like? If not, what is missing?

8. Sexuality

1. Have you ever been in a situation like Joseph's? How did you respond? How does this story illustrate fidelity?

2. Read 1 Corinthians 7:1-40 in sections. How have you heard this text interpreted in the past? Do you see it as a negative or positive portrayal of sexuality? Why?

3. What was your first thought when you read the title of this chapter? How is sexuality a metaphor for male spirituality?

4. Is celibacy an option that modern men should seriously consider? Why or why not? What can married men learn from celibate men and vice versa? How and why do they need each other?

5. Read Proverbs 5:15-19. How does this poem express fidelity? How can we express fidelity in various relationships? How is this related to our relationship with God?

9. Gifts

1. Joseph is a man with many gifts. How do you evaluate the progression from self to others in how he uses his gifts?

2. Read 1 Corinthians 12. What is the purpose of spiritual gifts? Why is diversity of gifts necessary? Do you agree with the author that biblical lists of gifts are not exhaustive? Why or why not? Which spiritual gifts do people say you have?

3. Read Acts 2:17-18. What does this mean for us today? How is this being fulfilled (or not) in the church today?

4. Why is it important for male spirituality to affirm gifts of leadership in women? What implications does this have for our spirituality?

5. How are men and women different (ignore the nature/nurture question)? How do men and women practice spiritual gifts differently?

10. Builder

1. What do you see as ordinary or extraordinary in Joseph's life as a builder? Which parts of his life can you identify with?

2. If you are married, reflect on the building of your marriage. How has God been a part of the everyday construction?

3. If you have children, where on the continuum of holding to letting go are you at present? How does this impact your spirituality?

4. If you are unmarried, what kind of blueprint do you envision for the building of your marriage and family, if those are in your plans and desires?

5. Read Colossians 3:17, 23-24. How is your work worship? How might a constant awareness of this change the way you work? How might it change you?

6. What is your view of money? How is money a spiritual thing, a god? What is the most important thing in your work?

7. How does it feel to realize you might be part of the most powerful people group on the planet? How can men use their power in an active and redemptive way?

8. How is competitiveness related to the previous themes of marriage, family, work, and money? How is it related to our spirituality? How can men cooperate through competition?

9. Read Exodus 20:8-11 and Deuteronomy 5:12-15.

Note the reasons for Sabbath-keeping in each text. How is the Sabbath principle related to the themes of the work, money, and competition?

11. Reflection

1. Who had the more traumatic look back, Joseph or his brothers? Why? How did they seem to have dealt with the separating incident in the ensuing years?

2. Read Ecclesiastes 11:7–12:7. What are the gifts/pleasures and the fears/temptations of each stage of life? What is the meaning (or meaninglessness) of life in each of these stages?

3. For those in midlife and beyond, what is there in your past that you might need to reflect on and process?

4. For those younger than midlife, what is there about getting older that excites you and/or terrifies you?

5. Which of the poems in this chapter could you best identify with or relate to: "Layers of Life," "Ghost Town," "Lost Boy," "Lost Boy, Found," 'The Ruins of St. Mary's Mission"? Why?

12. Reconciliation

1. What emotions do you feel at different points in the reconciliation narrative between Joseph and his brothers? What do you think of how the process happens?

2. Read 2 Corinthians 5:16-21. How does being in Christ give you a new and unique perspective on life? What does it mean to be "ambassadors" of reconciliation?

3. Have you ever experienced reconciliation after you were wronged or you had wronged someone else? Share some personal experiences.

4. Why do men have difficulty expressing emotions? How is this related to male friendship? What steps can we take toward emotional vulnerability and intimate friendship with other men?

5. How do you respond to the author's description of God? How would you describe the essence of God? If you only had one word or phrase to describe God, how would you describe God?

6. Our view of God gets at the heart of spirituality. What does our view of God say about the core of our spirituality? How do you respond to the author's final challenge to a more communal spirituality for men?

13. Legacy

1. Despite their failings and family dysfunctions, what legacy do Jacob and Joseph leave to their offspring?

2. Read John 13:1-17. How are Jesus' actions in this text a legacy for his disciples? What kind of legacy is he leaving? How is this exemplary for men?

3. How have you experienced the death and the funerals of those close to you? Share some stories.

4. What "death language" are you familiar with? What do you think of "gathered to his people" as describing death?

5. What's on your "bucket list"? How might shalom spirituality affirm or alter your bucket list? What kind of legacy will your bucket list leave for others?

NOTES

Chapter 1

1. All people mentioned in the book are real people but names and some details have been changed to protect their privacy.

2. Obviously, spirituality is a vast concept, but for our purposes, this brief definition will suffice at this time. It is based on the work of numerous theologians, from H. Richard Niebuhr to James Fowler.

3. Richard Rohr with Joseph Martos, *From Wild Man to Wise Man: Reflections on Male Spirituality* (Cincinnati, Ohio: St. Anthony Messenger Press, 2005), 88.

4. Ibid., 10. See also David Murrow, *Why Men Hate Going to Church* (Nashville: Thomas Nelson, 2005).

5. Although I have so far been using the terms men, male, and masculine interchangeably, we can differentiate these terms without having to become technical. *Male* describes gender or sexual difference. *Men* are adult males. *Masculine* describes character traits. While males have predominantly masculine traits and women feminine traits, males also have feminine traits and females masculine traits. Masculinity and femininity are both genetically and culturally determined. I will not explore arguments about what true masculinity or femininity is. My primary purpose is to describe a Christian spirituality for men, that is, adult males.

6. I echo the thoughts of Henri Nouwen in *Beloved: Spiritual Living in a Secular World* (New York: Crossroad, 1992), 20.

7. Richard Rohr, *Adam's Return: The Five Promises of Male Initiation* (New York: Crossroad, 2004), ix-x.

Chapter 2

1. Richard Rohr with Joseph Martos, *From Wild Man to Wise Man: Reflections on Male Spirituality* (Cincinnati, Ohio: St. Anthony Messenger Press, 2005), 148. Stu Webber, in his *Four Pillars of a Man's Heart* (Sisters, Ore.: Multnomah, 1997), calls them "pillars," but they are essentially the same thing as what most authors call "archetypes."

2. Robert Moore and Douglas Gillette, *King, Warrior, Magician, Lover: Rediscovering the Archetypes of Mature Masculinity* (San Francisco: HarperCollins, 1990).

3. The best recent example of the developmental view of the archetypes is John Eldredge's *The Way of the Wild Heart* (Nashville: Thomas Nelson, 2007). He uses them in this order but adds "the cowboy" as an archetype that comes before the warrior. This only adds to the caricature.

4. A good example is Stu Webber's illustration of the toppling pillars in *Four Pillars*, 63. The pillars that are meant for stability become unstable if they are out of balance.

5. John Eldredge, *Wild at Heart: Discovering the Secret to a Man's Soul* (Nashville: Thomas Nelson, 2001), 9.

6. Eldredge is very fond of Mel Gibson's movie *Braveheart* as an illustration of male spirituality. In fact, he thinks that Gibson's character, William Wallace, is more like Jesus than Mother Teresa (22).

7. See *Seven Promises of a Promise Keeper* (Colorado Springs: Focus on the Family, 1994) for a collection of articles explaining the basic principles of manhood encouraged by the organization. These promises also include reference to the other archetypes, although not in archetypal language.

8. Mark Driscoll, quoted by Mark Sayers on his blog

entry, "What does a redeemed masculinity look like?" www.marksayers.wordpress.com/2009/06/03

9. Paul Coughlin, *No More Christian Nice Guy* (Bloomington, Minn.: Bethany House, 2005), chaps. 1-3.

10. The words *pacifist* and *passive* are not etymologically related. They merely sound the same. Pacifists may be and have been passive in the past but are not necessarily so. A pacifist believes in "waging peace" and therefore could be said to be a "warrior *of* peace," but wholly unlike a warrior *for* peace, that is, one who wages a lethal war to try to achieve peace. The desired end is the same, but the pacifist believes that the means to the end of peace must be consistent with the end, that is, nonviolent peaceful means are the only way to achieve peace.

11. Military expert David Grossman discusses the psychology of killing in "Trained to Kill," *Christianity Today*, August 10, 1998.

Chapter 3

1. The quote from Mark Driscoll in the previous chapter illustrates this. Paul Coughlin's Jesus in *No More Christian Nice Guy* (Bloomington, Minn.: Bethany House, 2005), 30-45, is another example. He creates a Jesus that sounds more like a radio talk show host with a gift for "blessed sarcasm" than a first-century itinerant preacher. His point is true that we have often made Jesus into a nice, passive, middle-class American male, but his alternate caricature does not solve the problem.

2. William P. Young, *The Shack* (Newberry Park, Calif.: Windblown Media, 2007).

3. Philip Culbertson, *New Adam: The Future of Male Spirituality* (Minneapolis: Fortress Press, 1992).

4. Ibid., 12-13.

5. Richard Rohr with Joseph Martos, *From Wild Man*

to Wise Man: Reflections on Male Spirituality (Cincinnati, Ohio: St. Anthony Messenger Press, 2005), 45-52.

6. Eugene Peterson, *Leap Over a Wall: Earthy Spirituality for Everyday Christians* (New York: HarperCollins, 1997).

7. Exegetically, the Joseph text needs to be interpreted as a unit. The purpose of the story is to show the sovereign care of Yahweh for God's people. This overarching theme should be in the back of our minds as we explore the various specific metaphors. God is also with us on our journey.

8. Walter Brueggemann, *Praying the Psalms* (Winona, Minn.: St. Mary's Press, 1986), 34.

9. Consider gathering with others to discuss their own stories in a group. The branching out is then limited only by the imaginations of the participants. See the appendix for group discussion questions.

Chapter 4

1. Richard Rohr, *Adam's Return* (New York: Crossroad, 2004), 155.

2. Arthur Paul Boers, *Lord, Teach Us to Pray* (Waterloo, Ont.: Herald Press, 1992), 40.

3. This was a project of San Francisco Theological Seminary from 1997 to 2004. Its mission was "to foster Christian communities that are attentive to God's presence, discerning of the Spirit and who accompany young people into the way of Jesus." My brief explanation of the four movements is gleaned from a presentation entitled "The Theology of Contemplative Ministry," given by Michael Hryniuk on June 3, 2004, at San Francisco Theological Seminary, San Anselmo, California.

4. Donald Miller, *To Own a Dragon: Reflections on Growing up Without a Father* (Colorado Springs: NavPress, 2006), 62.

5. Henri Nouwen, *Beloved: Spiritual Living in a Secular World* (New York: Crossroad, 1992), 37-38.

6. William P. Young, *The Shack* (Newberry Park, Calif.: Windblown Media, 2007).

7. Nouwen, *Beloved*, 30.

Chapter 5

1. Morton Kelsey, *God, Dreams and Revelation* (Minneapolis: Augsburg Press, 1974), 4.

2. From Lloyd Lewis, *Myths after Lincoln* (New York: Grosset & Dunlap, 1957), as quoted in Louis M. Savary, Patricia H. Berne, and Stephon K. Williams, *Dreams and Spiritual Growth* (New York: Paulist Press, 1984), xi.

3. Kelsey, 7.

4. Sigmund Freud, *The Interpretation of Dreams* (New York: Random House, 1950), chap. 1.

5. Lyle E. Bourne Jr. and Bruce R. Ekstrand, *Psychology: Its Principles and Meanings* (New York: Holt, Rinehart and Winston, 1982), 520.

6. Walter Wink, *The Powers that Be* (New York: Doubleday, 1998), 187.

7. The most recent fuller treatment of these stages can be found in James Fowler, *Becoming Adult, Becoming Christian* (San Francisco: Jossey-Bass, 2001), 40-57.

8. I first encountered this term in James Fowler's writings. I like it as an inclusive and descriptive paraphrase of "kingdom of God."

9. Martin Luther King Jr., *I Have a Dream: Writings and Speeches That Changed the World*, ed. James Melvin Washington (San Francisco: HarperSanFrancisco, 1992), 104-5.

Chapter 6

1. "Everybody Hurts" from the album *Automatic for the People* by R.E.M., Columbia Records, 1992.

2. Henri Nouwen, *The Wounded Healer* (New York: Doubleday, 1972), 88.

3. Richard Rohr with Joseph Martos, *From Wild Man to Wise Man: Reflections on Male Spirituality* (Cincinnati, Ohio: St. Anthony Messenger Press, 2005), chaps. 11, 12.

4. Ibid., 77.

5. Donald Miller, *To Own a Dragon: Reflections on Growing up Without a Father* (Colorado Springs: NavPress, 2006).

6. Rohr, *From Wild Man to Wiseman*, 73-74.

7. Ibid., 77.

Chapter 7

1. Erik Erikson, *Identity: Youth and Crisis* (New York: Norton, 1968), 157.

2. John Eldredge, *Wild at Heart: Discovering the Secret to a Man's Soul* (Nashville: Thomas Nelson, 2001), chap. 11, and *The Way of the Wild Heart* (Nashville: Thomas Nelson, 2007), chaps. 5-6, for excellent stories and articulation of this metaphor.

3. One that has been particularly meaningful for me is J. Nelson Kraybill's *On Pilgrim's Way* (Waterloo: Herald Press, 1999).

4. Arthur Paul Boers, "One Pilgrim's Progress," *Canadian Mennonite*, May 26, 2008, 6. The article is adapted from his book, *The Way Is Made by Walking* (Downer's Grove, Ill.: InterVarsity Press, 2007).

Chapter 8

1. Richard Rohr with Joseph Martos, *From Wild Man to Wise Man: Reflections on Male Spirituality* (Cincinnati, Ohio: St. Anthony Messenger Press, 2005), 75.

2. Rob Bell, *Sex God* (Grand Rapids: Zondervan, 2007), 42, 40.

3. See Paul Coughlin, *No More Christian Nice Guy* (Bloomington, Minn.: Bethany House, 2005), 95-102, for an example of this attitude.

4. Although sexual orientation may also contribute to a unique spirituality, that is beyond the scope of this chapter. I believe the descriptions of fidelity in this chapter apply equally regardless of sexual orientation.

5. Ted Grimsrud and Mark Thiessen Nation, *Reasoning Together: A Conversation on Homosexuality* (Scottdale, Pa.: Herald Press, 2008), 249.

6. Jana Bennett, "Support for Celibate Singles Alongside Monogamous Married Couples and Their Children," in Rutba House, ed., *School(s) for Conversion: 12 Marks of a New Monasticism* (Eugene, Ore.: Cascade Books, 2005), 115.

7. Lewis B. Smedes, *Sex for Christians* (Grand Rapids: Eerdmans, 1976), 134.

8. Donald Miller, *To Own a Dragon: Reflections on Growing up Without a Father* (Colorado Springs: NavPress, 2006), 141.

9. Shane Claiborne is a well-traveled activist and speaker who has also authored several books, including *The Irresistible Revolution* (Grand Rapids: Zondervan, 2006) and, most recently, *Jesus for President* (Grand Rapids: Zondervan, 2008).

10. Bennett, 114.

11. Ibid., 118.

12. Ibid., 115.

Chapter 9

1. L. Hyde as quoted in Kester Brewin, *Signs of Emergence* (Grand Rapids: Baker, 2007), 163.

2. Sally Morgenthaler, "Leadership in a Flattened World," in Tony Jones and Doug Pagitt, eds., *An Emergent Manifesto of Hope* (Grand Rapids: Baker, 2007), 188.

3. The four scales are (1) energy source: introversion/extraversion, (2) gathering information: senses/intuition, (3) making decisions: thinking/feeling, (4) life orientation: perceiving/judging. There has been a lot of good research done with the Myers-Briggs and its relationship to giftedness and gender.

4. There is a statistical research difference, but that does not mean all men and women are like this. I prefer the feeling mode, for example, and some women prefer the thinking. A preference also does not indicate that men do not feel or that women do not think, just a general preference for how decisions are processed. Some decisions call for one or the other preference, and both genders can learn to use both preferences when appropriate. See Isabel Briggs Myers with Peter B. Myers, *Gifts Differing: Understanding Personality Type* (Palo Alto, Calif.: Davies Black Publishing, 1995), 34, 66.

Chapter 10

1. John Eldredge claims that all men have three deep desires, one being to rescue a beautiful woman. See *Wild at Heart: Discovering the Secret to a Man's Soul* (Nashville: Nelson, 2001), 9.

2. Ernest Boyer Jr., *Finding God at Home: Family Life as a Spiritual Discipline* (San Francisco: Harper & Row, 1988), 17.

3. Ibid., 65.

4. Ibid., 67.

5. Fred H. Kaan, "Worship the Lord," words Copyright © 1974 by Hope Publishing Company, Carol Stream, Ill. (www.hopepublishing.com).

6. From "Seventh Book," in *Aurora Leigh*, by Elizabeth Barrett Browning.

7. Richard Rohr with Joseph Martos, *From Wild Man to Wise Man: Reflections on Male Spirituality* (Cincinnati, Ohio: St. Anthony Messenger Press, 2005), 60.

8. Ibid., 61.

9. Leonard Beechy, *The Meaning of Tough: Wealth and Power* (Waterloo, Ont.: Faith & Life Resources, 2003), 10.

10. Ibid., 14.

11. I first heard this story from my colleague Erv Klassen, who pointed me to Cornelia Lehn, *Peace Be with You* (Newton, Kan.: Faith & Life Press, 1980).

12. Ray Gingerich, "The Canons of Anabaptism: Which Anabaptism? Whose Canon?" in Alain Epp Weaver and Gerald J. Mast, eds., *The Work of Jesus Christ in Anabaptist Perspective* (Telford, Penn.: Cascadia Press, 2008), 200-1.

13. "Study: Women not much into pro sports," *The Province* (Vancouver, B.C.), August 31, 2009, A46. This article quotes a study by Canadian sociologist Reginald Bibby of the University of Lethbridge.

14. J. Denny Weaver, "Christian faith and athletics: or can a true Mennonite enjoy football?" *Bluffton*, Summer 2003, 12.

15. David Murrow, *Why Men Hate Going to Church* (Nashville: Nelson, 2005).

Chapter 11

1. This process will be described in the next chapter.

Chapter 12

1. For Tom Fox's story in greater detail, see James Loney, "No Greater Love," in Tricia Gates Brown, ed., *118 Days: Christian Peacemaker Teams Held Hostage in Iraq* (Toronto: Christian Peacemaker Teams, 2008), 203-20.

2. David Grossman, "Trained to Kill," *Christianity Today*, August 10, 1998.

3. "Real Men Cry" is a song by Terry Scott Taylor as recorded by the Lost Dogs on the album *Real Men Cry* (Zoom Daddy Music, 2001).

4. In *The Scandal of the Cross* (Downers Grove, Ill.: InterVarsity Press, 2000), authors Joel B. Green and Mark D. Baker, point out that the Bible contains a variety of metaphors and that we should not restrict ourselves to just one way of speaking about the atonement.

5. For an extensive treatment of this view of the atonement, see J. Denny Weaver, *The Nonviolent Atonement* (Grand Rapids, Mich.: Eerdmans, 2001).

6. James Fowler, *Becoming Adult, Becoming Christian* (San Francisco: Jossey-Bass, 2001), 35.

Chapter 13

1. Eugene Peterson in the introduction to the book of Ezekiel, *The Message Remix* (Colorado Springs: NavPress, 2003), 1,494.

2. Many biblical references could be given here, but a few of my favorites are Isaiah 40; Philippians 2:6-11; Colossians 1:20.

3. *The Bad News Bears* is a movie about a boys' baseball team made up of a ragtag variety of misfits and losers who, in the classic underdog movie script, eventually come together as a team and win the championship.

Epilogue

1. Adapted and reformatted from Rainer Maria Rilke, "Letters to a Young Poet" (Novato, Calif.: New World Library, 2000), 35.

THE AUTHOR

Gareth Brandt cycles to work in Abbotsford, British Columbia, where he teaches practical theology at Columbia Bible College. His educational background includes degrees in spirituality, theology, and psychology, with an emphasis on the spiritual formation of young adults. He has a background in congregational and denominational youth ministry.

Gareth is married to Cynthia, an elementary school teacher, and they have four children ages 19, 17, 15, and 8. They are active members of Emmanuel Mennonite Church in Abbotsford. The family enjoys participating in music, drama, and other creative pursuits.

Gareth was born in Steinbach, Manitoba, and grew up on a small farm in western Manitoba. He has been writing poetry since he was a teenager and has published various articles in journals and magazines. This is his first book on a subject he never thought he'd write about. Gareth is passionate about helping people to discover, articulate, and develop their personal spirituality.

CPSIA information can be obtained at www.ICGtesting.com
Printed in the USA
BVOW011405221012

303520BV00007B/3/P

9 780836 195026